Gunther Plüschow

Gunther Plüschow

Airman, Escaper, Explorer

The Remarkable Story of the Only German POW
Ever to Escape from Britain

Anton Rippon

Pen & Sword
MILITARY

First published in Great Britain in 2009 by
Pen & Sword Military
an imprint of
Pen & Sword Books Ltd
47 Church Street
Barnsley
South Yorkshire
S70 2AS

ISBN 978 1 84884 132 1

A CIP catalogue record for this book is
available from the British Library

Typeset in Ehrhardt by Phoenix Typesetting, Auldgirth, Dumfriesshire

Printed and bound in England by the MPG Books Group

Pen & Sword Books Ltd incorporates the imprints of Pen & Sword Aviation, Pen & Sword Maritime, Pen & Sword Military, Wharncliffe Local History, Pen & Sword Select, Pen & Sword Military Classics and Leo Cooper.

For a complete list of Pen & Sword titles please contact
PEN & SWORD BOOKS LIMITED
47 Church Street, Barnsley, South Yorkshire, S70 2AS, England
E-mail: enquiries@pen-and-sword.co.uk
Website: www.pen-and-sword.co.uk

Contents

Preface

My interest in Gunther Plüschow began all of thirty years ago when I read an account of a German prisoner of war whose escape from a British POW camp involved him catching a train from Derby, where I lived, to London from where he eventually made it all the way home. He was the only German prisoner in either world war to do that (forget Franz von Werra, immortalized in the film *The One That Got Away*; his eventual escape was made over the Canadian border to the then neutral USA) but it was the Derby connection that made me take more interest in Gunther Plüschow than I might otherwise have done.

When I began to look further into his life, I was astounded. Plüschow's was the sort of story that John Buchan might have written – there were even hints that Gunther Plüschow might have been a spy – and eventually, when time would allow from other commitments, I knew that I would have to put it all together.

What follows here is, I believe, the first full account of Gunther Plüschow's astonishing life, from cradle to grave, to be published in a single volume, one that now also contains new and updated information not easily available to earlier researchers.

Names are spelled as they were at the time, so Peking is still Peking, not Beijing. Similarly, under the modern Pinyin system Tsingtao (properly pronounced as 'Ching-Dao') is now Qingdao but I have stuck with the English spelling at the time these events took place (the Germans spelled it Tsingtau, hence the name of Plüschow's Heinkel). German military ranks are given their British equivalents.

Anton Rippon,
Derby, England
Summer 2009

vii

Acknowledgements

OVER the years (as far back as 1916 in fact) several books, some of them written by Gunther Plüschow himself, and at least one by his wife, have dealt with particular aspects of his story. Without these, and without the tireless and inestimable research of authors such as Robert E Whittaker and Roberto Litvachkes, and the work of people like Gerhard H Ehlers and his colleagues whose *Freundeskreis Gunther Plüschow* travelling exhibition helps keep Plüschow's memory alive, this book would have been all the more difficult to write. Full details may be found in the Bibliography. Special thanks must go to Hanni Dove and Nicola Rippon for their translations of German documents into English; to Arthur Shardlow of Castle Donington for additional information about the prison camp there; to Uwe Porten (www.genealogy-germany.de), a genealogical researcher based in Germany who several times pointed me in the right direction and was most generous with his advice; to Gerhard Mesli of the Landesarchiv Berlin who searched out details of Gunther Plüschow's final resting place; and Bernhard Weidemann of the Deutsches Museum in Munich who gave advice on photographs.

List of Plates

The proud young naval officer: Gunther Plüschow in 1906.

SMS *Fürst Bismarck*, the flagship on which Gunther Plüschow first served on the China Station.

A little bit of Germany by the sea: Tsingtao pictured on the eve of the First World War.

German officers horse racing at Tsingtao. Gunther Plüschow had to use the racecourse as a makeshift airfield.

Japanese forces land at Laoshan Bay to the north of Tsingtao in September 1914.

Plüschow's Rumpler Taube outside the walls of Haichow.

Plüschow presents the engine of the Taube to the local mandarin at Haichow.

A sad moment: Plüschow with his burning Taube.

Plüschow poses in the clothes he wore during his escape from London.

Mr McGarvin on board the *Mongolia* as it reaches the United States.

The liner *Andania* was used as a prison ship in the Solent. It was Gunther Plüschow's first 'home' when he arrived in England.

A newspaper artist's impressions of life at Dorchester POW camp in 1915.

German prisoners attract much attention as they are marched through the streets of Castle Donington on their way to Donington Hall in 1915.

Donington Hall camp, a stately home surrounded by a wire fence.

German officers enjoy a game of football in the shadow of their Donington prison.

Two German officers engrossed in a game of chess at Donington Hall.

Gunther Plüschow and Isot are married in an aircraft hanger at Libau in June 1916.

Gunther Plüschow hosts a visit by the Kaiserin, Princess Auguste Viktoria, to the air base at Kiel-Holtenau in 1916.

A portrait of Gunther Plüschow taken in 1930 before he returned to South America for the last time.

The *Feuerland* that took Plüschow and his party halfway around the world.

The Heinkel HD 24W – the *Silberkondor* – pictured in the bay at Ushuaia.

The *Silberkondor* in the harbour at Punta Arenas, December 1928.

Ernst Dreblow, pictured at a base camp in Patagonia.

The *Silberkondor* dwarfed by its surroundings.

Newspaper cutting reporting the interment of Gunther Plüschow's ashes at the Park Cemetery in the Berlin suburb of Lichterfelde.

The legend lives on: advertisement for the film *Ikarus* that was released after Plüschow's death.

Prologue

On 12 December 2006, in the Chilean city of Punta Arenas – 'the southernmost city on Earth' – a group of people gathered before a monument at the end of the wide Avenida Cristóbel Colón overlooking the Strait of Magellan. Behind the monument, the crowning feature of which was an anchor, the flags of Germany, Chile, and of the Magellan Region and Chilean Antarctica, fluttered in the stiff breeze of a southern summer. Several VIPs were present, among them Juan Morano, the Mayor of Punta Arenas; Monsignor Bernardo Bastres Florence, the recently appointed Bishop of Punta Arenas; General Federico Klock of the Chilean Air Force; Eduardo Cano, Director of the city's German School; and an eminent historian, Professor Mateo Martinic, Director of the Patagonian Institute at the University of Magellan. Looking on at the area that would henceforth be known as the Plazoleta (the Spanish word for small square) Gunther Plüschow were pupils from the local German School, citizens of Punta Arenas and several journalists there to record the occasion. As the ceremony unfolded, a military chaplain blessed the monument.

From the civil authority, from the church, from the military, from academe, and from the ordinary man, woman and child in the streets, they had come to honour a very special man, someone who had made a major contribution to their region. Because of that contribution, Argentina also remembered him: in October 2007 a ceremony would be held in his honour in the Parliament building in Buenos Aires. The previous year there had even been plans to build a Gunther Plüschow theme park in Argentina. The Gunther Plüschow Glacier ('awe-inspiring, breathtakingly beautiful') in Tierra del Fuego, a highlight on the itinerary of any liner cruising in the region, is also named in memory of him. And in his native Germany, from September 1931 onwards, streets in

1

several towns and cities, large and small, have been renamed for him. He is a legend there, too, although for very different reasons. They remember his courage during the First World War. Seventy-five years before the ceremony in Punta Arenas, there had been a huge gathering in Berlin as his ashes were laid to rest.

So who was this man who is held in such high esteem by people from disparate nations and whose reputation survived another world war and several generations. Who was Gunther Plüschow?

Chapter 1

'Fulfil This Goal'

Gunther Plüschow could boast royal blood – and a slightly convoluted family tree. His grandfather, Carl Friedrich Eduard Plüschow, a high-ranking civil servant at the court of Grand Duke Friedrich Franz II of Mecklenburg-Schwerin, a grand duchy in northern Germany, was an illegitimate son of Hereditary Grand Duke Friedrich Ludwig, who had pre-deceased his father, Grand Duke Friedrich Franz I.

Gunther was born in Munich on the fine winter's day of 8 February 1886. His father, Eduard Plüschow, had some interesting siblings. Among Eduard's two brothers and four sisters were Anna, who became a painter, and Wilhelm, the eldest, who went to Italy to work as a photographer, mostly taking pictures of nude youths. Wilhelm was apparently the black sheep of the family: he became known as Guglielmo Plüschow and eventually returned to Berlin in 1910 after several scandals, one of which resulted in his spending eight months in prison after being found guilty of corrupting minors. The Plüschows were certainly a colourful lot.

As for Gunther's father, after a disappointing and short-lived military career Eduard Plüschow became a journalist and in 1875 moved to Rome to work. He returned to Germany in 1880 and married Hermione Wellensiek, daughter of a well-known cigar manufacturer from the Westphalian town of Bünde, but after Gunther's birth he took the family back to Rome where the youngster grew up among the bustle of street traders, students and festivals of that vibrant city. His parents loved mixing with Rome's artistic community – Gunther had been named after a character in Richard Wagner's *Der Ring des Nibelungen* – and

3

every day painters, writers, artists and musicians gathered around the Plüschows' large dining table at their home in a colourful neighbourhood on one of Rome's hills.

Young Gunther enjoyed the freedom to explore this wonderful, sunny, always exciting city. The mischievous child, 'the blond devil' as the neighbours called him, could often be seen undertaking some commercial enterprise or other, often peddling junk that he and his brother Hans, who was three years older, had found lying around the streets. Gunther's fledgling business career came to an end when he was enrolled in a French Jesuit school, where he excelled, especially in languages.

When Eduard fell ill, the family moved back to Germany, to the hometown of Gunther's mother. Bünde, which became known as 'the Cigar Box of Germany', was a small town on the River Else between Bielefeld and Hanover. When he had recovered, Gunther's father became a curator at the Department of Prints and Drawings of the newly opened State Art Museum in Schwerin, the capital of Mecklenburg-Schwerin, located about 50 miles south of the Baltic Sea and surrounded by picturesque lakes. Schwerin Castle, for centuries the residence of the dukes and grand dukes of Mecklenburg and later Mecklenburg-Schwerin, stood in the middle of one of the biggest, the Schweriner See.

The Plüschows settled into a fine old house amid the forest on the edge of what was Eduard's native town. Gunther, in particular, enjoyed his new surroundings. He soon made new friends. They were mostly his own age but the one friendship he probably treasured most was that of an aged sailor who taught him sailing. Young boy and elderly man, they looked an unlikely couple, skimming across the water in the old salt's treasured gig, a fast, light rowing boat.

Alas, for Gunther Plüschow those glorious days were to end all too soon. In April 1896, the 10-year-old took the first faltering steps of his military career. Leaving the idyllic life of Schwerin behind him, he followed in the footsteps of his brother, Hans, and entered the cadet institute at Plön, a small town 19 miles from the great German naval base of Kiel. A younger brother, Wolfgang who was born in 1888, would also serve in the military.

Plön lay on Schleswig-Holstein's biggest lake, the Grosser Plöner See, as well as on several smaller lakes that touched the town on virtually all sides. On a hill overlooking the town, the Schloss Plön, a magnificent stately home built in the seventeenth century, housed the cadet school that catered for boys aged between 10 and 15. The former summer residence of a Danish king, Christian VIII, after the German–Danish war of 1864, Schloss Plön had fallen into Prussian hands and in 1868 it became home to the school that could boast the sons of Kaiser Wilhelm II among its pupils. Set amid lakes, forests and mountains, Plön fired still further young Gunther's passion for nature and the outdoors.

Like all other aspiring new students on that spring day, he had first to undergo a rudimentary physical examination followed by the common entrance examination. Then the newcomers ate a meal together (their parents, formally dressed, waited separately) while the exams were marked and the students graded before fees had to be paid. If the first day was a particular ordeal for the new boys, it was something of a holiday for the old hands who were given a rare day off when new cadets arrived for their induction.

Young Plüschow was one of the brightest of his intake – he had already been brought forward at his preparatory school – and there was no doubt that he would soon be wearing the cadets' drab uniform of simple unadorned tunic, grey shirt and black tie. The underwear was uncomfortable and there were also the fatigues. On special occasions, however, the boys could don their dress tunics with red shoulder straps and cuff facings common to all cadet lower schools but with the white piping unique to Plön.

Naturally, the academy at Plön utilized its location to the full and students enjoyed ample opportunities to test their skills on the water, from rowing boats to piloting small military craft. Plüschow took to it all like the proverbial duck. He excelled at swimming and also won a place on the rowing team. In addition, he became absorbed in the military history of his country, an interest that was fed when a tutor took parties of students on visits to places like Kiel which was still growing at a furious pace, to the port town of Sonderburg, and especially to Duppel that had played a conspicuous part in the mid-nineteenth-century conflicts between the Germans and the Danes.

In 1900, Plüschow said goodbye to the lower cadet school at Plön and hello to the next stage of his education. After German unification in 1871 each new Army Bill had seen renewed calls for expansion and, with it, the obvious need for more officers. Lower cadet schools had been added and in 1878, to accommodate the growing number of students these schools were producing, a new facility for senior cadets – the Imperial Military Academy – had been built at Gross-Lichterfelde, 6 miles southwest of Berlin, on the rail line to Potsdam. The original senior academy had stood in the older part of Berlin, on the Friedrichstrasse between the Alexanderplatz and the Jarowitz Bridge. It had been built along classical lines by Frederick the Great, but eventually the lack of facilities, especially exercise space, saw the move to the Gross-Lichterfelde estate where there was every modern convenience, although new students were immediately reminded of the reasons for their being there. Above the main entrance to the administration building stood bronze statues of Frederick Wilhelm I, Frederick the Great, Frederick Wilhelm III and Kaiser Wilhelm I, while marble busts of the heroes of the Seven Years' War lined the grand entrance hall.

Writing in 1933, Ernst von Salomon, who was a student at Karlsruhe before going on to Gross-Lichterfelde, recalled his first days at cadet school, particularly the speech given by a young lieutenant:

You have chosen the finest profession that there is on earth. You have the highest goal in sight . . . We teach you here to fulfill this goal. You are here about to learn what confers significance first to last on your life. You are here to learn about death. From now on you no longer have free will; you will have to learn to obey, later to be able to command . . .

The 14-year-old Gunther Plüschow would have gone to bed with similar words ringing in his ears.

By the time Plüschow arrived at Gross-Lichterfelde it was home to 1,000 students, quite a difference to the 160 with whom he had rubbed shoulders at Plön. And unlike Plön, with its campus-like layout in extensive open park-like grounds, the 109-acre site at Gross-Lichterfelde comprised eighteen buildings, including four big barrack blocks with a dining hall that could seat 1,000 cadets at the same time, a church and the administration building, all surrounded by three large yards, an exercise field, and a parade ground that was overlooked by a huge statue, the Flensburg Lion, originally intended as a monument of the Danish victory over Schleswig-Holstein in 1850 but taken to Berlin by the Prussians after the German victory of 1864. The central buildings especially felt more like an army barracks, a fortress even, surrounded on all sides by thick 10ft-high walls.

Plüschow may have escaped much of the physical abuse reserved by older boys for newcomers. As someone who had graduated from one of the cadet lower schools, he would have been assumed to have already suffered his fair share. Von Salomon, for instance, recalled his own rite of passage: 'Glasmacher took my head in his hands, pressed me in the eyes and forced my skull hard to the table top . . . then whizzed the first blow . . . after that they rained down on the back, shoulders, legs'.

At the end of his first year at Gross-Lichterfelde, Gunther Plüschow had decided on where his future lay and he was accepted on the academy's naval navigation course. The story goes that, with a group of fellow cadets who were also showing an interest in the navy, he formed a sort of 'Sailors' Club' whose members pored over maps and travel books in the Imperial Military Academy's library, then planned dream trips to faraway places with strange-sounding names. On one such occasion, Plüschow was studying a book on South America when he came across some illustrations of Tierra del Fuego, the 150-mile long archipelago separated from the South American mainland by the Strait of Magellan. Ice-packed misty mountain peaks, large glaciers pouring down into the sea, beautiful forests, lakes, fast rivers and waterfalls, abundant bird life – to Plüschow this might have been Paradise itself, although the exquisite beauty of the region hid from a wide-eyed young man the realities of its harsh climate. None the less, Plüschow is reputed to have torn the illustrations from the book, telling his colleagues: 'You have nothing to do with it. This one is my country.'

Chapter 2

China Station

So the navy was to be his career and Gunther Plüschow's time at Gross-Lichterfelde came to an end. In April 1904, he was sent to the SMS *Stosch*, a three-masted fully rigged training ship for officers that had been launched in October 1877 from the yard of AG Vulcan at Stettin (now the Polish city of Szczecin). A previous cadet serving on the *Stosch* had been Erich Raeder, the man who under Hitler would become a grand admiral, the first person to hold that rank since Alfred von Tirpitz. Every day before breakfast, Raeder and his fellow cadets had to race to the top of the mizzenmast, the aftermost of the ship's trio of masts, and then back down within fifty-eight seconds. After he had been ranked fourth out of thirty-five cadets to do this, he was shifted on to the much higher mainmast, with the same task to be performed but in one minute and three seconds. Whether this particular endurance test was still being practised when Plüschow stepped aboard the *Stosch*, four years after Raeder had bid her farewell, is not recorded, but discipline was certainly still harsh.

Plüschow, though, enjoyed the hands-on experience of learning practical seamanship. Aside from handling sail, cadets learned rowing and sailing in the cutters, gun drill on antiquated 15cm guns, navigation, seamanship, English, French and mathematics. Of course, Plüschow was a star pupil: his basic seamanship learned on the lake at Plön stood him in good stead; he was already a good linguist having spent part of his childhood outside Germany; and his all-round academic achievements had seen him moved ahead of his year at both his preparatory school and at Plön.

The discomforts aboard the *Stosch* might have been tiresome – his 'bedroom' was nothing more than a hammock, a mattress and two blankets – but the experience of 'roughing it' would serve him well in years to come. As expected, after a year on the board the training ship Plüschow passed his final examinations with flying colours. That he was on a short holiday in Brussels when he received the news of his success underlined the fact that the desire to travel was already eating away at him.

It was an itch that he was soon able to scratch. Sent back to Schleswig-Holstein, to the port of Flensburg, Plüschow found himself posted to the torpedo boat *S-87* before, in October 1906, joining the Norddeutscher Lloyd mail ship, *Prinzregent Luitpold*, at Hamburg for a seven-week voyage to the Far East, where he was to join Germany's first armoured cruiser and the flagship of the East Asia Squadron, the vessel that became known as SMS *Fürst Bismarck* which was based at Tsingtao, a German protectorate on the Chinese mainland.

The *Prinzregent Luitpold*, whose ultimate destination was Yokohama, called at Southampton, then Gibraltar, Genoa, Naples, Port Said, Colombo and Singapore, where Plüschow was joined by a party of fellow cadets before they sailed on together to Shanghai, from where they were to complete their journey on the Hamburg-Amerika Line's steamer, *Admiral Tirpitz*. It was late November when they arrived at China's gateway to the Western world and the cadets spent a few days' leave in the 'international' city with its reputation for intrigue and danger. Plüschow found the place to his liking; it was like living in the pages of a thriller novel, he remarked. Inevitably, there was an adventure: together with a chef from Berlin called Richard Neumann, who was working in Shanghai, he helped to rescue an absent sailor from an opium den and smuggled him back on to his ship.

In the spring of 1907, now already well established aboard the *Fürst Bismarck*, Plüschow had his first taste of Japan as the ship paid goodwill visits to several ports. Ever interested in other lands and other cultures, he took time to explore the Japanese

Cherry Blossom Festival tradition. The *Fürst Bismarck* sailed on through the Tsushima Strait that connects the Sea of Japan and the East China Sea, surveying the area where, two years earlier, one of the most decisive naval battles in history had been fought when the Japanese all but destroyed the Russian fleet. Plüschow's ship paid what was billed as a courtesy visit to the former Russian naval base at Port Arthur; in fact the visit enabled the Germans to study Japanese defences there. Twelve years earlier, the Japanese ambassador to Berlin had told Germany that his country would demand Port Arthur and the Liaotung Peninsula 'as a sort of Gibraltar for the Gulf of Petschili'. The storm clouds that would forever change the life of Gunther Plüschow had been gathering for a long time. Meanwhile, on an excursion to the Chinese mainland he joined fellow officers on a visit to the Great Wall of China.

Plüschow's time aboard the *Fürst Bismarck* as she sailed around on her East Asian duties certainly fed his appetite for an escapade, for pleasure – and for the occasional argument. When a British steamer, the Imperial Direct West India Mail Service Company's SS *Port Maria*, which, as its company's name implies, was more usually found on the West Indies run, was experiencing some mechanical fault below the waterline, the ever-resourceful Plüschow donned diving gear and sorted out the problem in next to no time.

A round of parties in Manila introduced him to members of the Italian and American communities as well as to ex-patriot Germans working there. These were pleasant evenings as the *Fürst Bismarck*'s officers mingled with civilians who were excited to meet these dashing men in naval uniform. In Batavia (now Jakarta), the officers were entertained at Tanah Abang, at the home of Emil Helfferich, a German entrepreneur who had made plenty of money in the pepper trade. Helfferich was quite a character – he was also a poet – who had spent a year in the artillery before becoming a merchant. He had once tried to enlist in the navy but poor eyesight thwarted that ambition, and he was always ready to talk to seafarers. Later that day, the men from the

Fürst Bismarck were treated to a rowdy evening of drinking and pony racing at the Harmonie Club.

It was in Batavia, then the capital of the Dutch East Indies, that there was a less pleasant note when Gunther Plüschow exchanged heated words with a Dutch government official over the Netherlands' colonial policies; the young German naval officer was becoming politically aware.

By June 1909 the *Fürst Bismarck* had been replaced as the East Asia Squadron's flagship by SMS *Scharnhorst* and was back in Kiel undergoing a refit, never to return to front-line action. It was to serve as a training ship and administrative centre before being withdrawn from service in 1919 and scrapped a year later. Like the *Fürst Bismarck* Plüschow's time on the China Station was also coming to an end and in 1910 he returned to Germany on the Norddeutscher Lloyd steamer SS *Lützow* that, in August 1914, would be captured by the British and spend the First World War serving them as the troopship *Huntsend*. Gunther climbed aboard the *Lützow* with one permanent souvenir: a tattoo of a dragon that ran from his left shoulder down to his forearm, mostly in green but with a small amount of blue and red.

Back in Hamburg, Plüschow, now a lieutenant, applied to be posted back to *S-87*. As he waited for an answer, he got himself attached to the Kaiser Friedrich III class battleship SMS *Kaiser Barbarossa* in order to take a diving course. Around this time, however, there were two family tragedies. In April 1910, Gunther received a letter from his sister, Carlotta, telling him that their mother was seriously ill in a Berlin hospital. The family managed to gather at her bedside before she died on 2 May that year; she was buried in Bünde, alongside her own mother and father. On 14 November 1911, Eduard Plüschow died suddenly at the family home in Schwerin. Within eighteen months, Gunther had lost both parents.

As he came to terms with these devastating blows, his application to rejoin *S-87* was approved, but just as he was immersing himself in his duties there, the torpedo boat was withdrawn from service because a new class of smaller, faster boats was being introduced.

Plüschow now found himself on an eighteen-month posting as an inspecting officer at the recently opened Imperial German Naval Academy at Mürwik on the Flensburg Fjord. The academy had originally been established at Kiel but the rapid expansion of the German Navy meant that facilities there no longer satisfied the growing demand for officers, and between 1907 and 1910, the imposing building with its North German Gothic façade and 200ft-high tower grew to dominate a 37-acre site on the southern shore of the bay. The north and south wings housed accommodation blocks. The east wing was used for class-rooms, administration offices and a gymnasium. At the official inauguration on 21 November 1910, Kaiser Wilhelm II addressed the cadets and issued the Cabinet Order listing prior-ities for officer training. The naval officer should be 'an educated man in a general sense . . . with broad technical knowledge'. First and foremost, however, naval leadership should be about person-ality and character. The 'red brick castle by the sea', as Mürwik came to be known, was Germany's equivalent of the Royal Naval College at Dartmouth or the United States Naval Academy at Annapolis.

By 1912, Flensburg was a busy centre of trade and industry, and Germany's third largest port city after Hamburg and Bremen. There was a host of industries, such as breweries, distilleries, cloth and paper factories, glass-works, copper-works, soap-works and rice mills, but it was the sea that dominated. There were shipbuilding yards and excellent wharves that served commercial interests including Greenland whaling and oyster fisheries. And besides the Mürwik academy there were schools of marine engineering and navigation.

All in all, Flensburg seemed just the place to satisfy the crav-ings of a young man devoted to a life at sea. But then Gunther Plüschow began to become aware of the fledgling science of aviation.

Chapter 3

Dove of War

In August 1913, Gunther Plüschow returned to Schwerin. In many ways, it had been a strange summer for him. On a visit to Rome he had bumped into a young woman called Elsa Kempfer, originally from Magdeburg, whom he had known in Berlin. Three years younger than Gunther, she was known as Isot and they spent several days walking the streets of the Eternal City. And they fell in love. But Gunther had other distractions. He had applied to train as a flyer in the Imperial Navy's fledgling aviation section. Later that summer, he spent a few weeks in England, wandering around London, taking in the sights and visiting museums and art galleries. It was a world he knew well from his father's post in Schwerin. Yet there was only one thing on his mind. The naval list of autumn promotions should have been published and he was bursting to know whether he had been accepted on the aviation course.

Now he was back and an uncle collected him from the railway station. The uncle, who was well connected and a man of some influence, had good news for Gunther: 'Congratulations – you've been posted to the Naval Flying Corps.' Plüschow wrote later that it was all he could do to refrain from turning a somersault in the middle of the street.

The last few days of his leave sped by, and then he returned to Mürwik to finish his time there before packing his belongings and waiting for news of the flying course. Before he left the Naval Academy for the last time, he was given some further news. A fellow officer asked him if he knew where he was to be posted.

'Yes,' said Plüschow, 'the Flying Corps.'

'I know that,' said his colleague, 'but you're going to Tsingtao.'

If he had thought about performing a somersault at the news that he was going to be an aviator, then the thought of returning to the Far East, and to Tsingtao in particular, made him want to cartwheel all the way down Mürwik's main avenue. It was to be a three-year posting on the China Station but first he had to qualify as a flying man.

He had to be patient; first there were three months to be spent at Kiel. But on 1 January 1914, Lieutenant Gunther Plüschow of the Imperial German Navy reported to Germany's first-ever commercial airfield at Johannisthal, 10 miles south-east of Berlin.

Opened on 26 September 1909, Johannisthal was ostensibly a private facility that the military subsidized to the tune of 20,000 marks a year. The German War Ministry had been an early supporter of the possibilities of aviation and as early as 1900 had financially supported both the Berlin Aviation Association and the Imperial Aero Club. The government's own airfield facility was the next logical step and the subsidy to the company that had set up Johannisthal was a cheap way of achieving it. A military flying school was also set up at Döberitz in 1910, and in April 1911 the Inspection of Military Air and Motorized Automobile Service was formed to explore the use of the new technologies of motorcar and aircraft engines for military purposes. This, though, was largely the responsibility of a transportation unit; the military thinking was still that aviation was for transport and observation not combat. The Imperial German Navy had taken an early interest in the subject and had begun seaplane research in 1911, although Grand Admiral Prince Heinrich, the Kaiser's younger brother, was an ardent champion of naval aviation and in the Baltic he would use seaplanes for torpedo attack and aerial mine-laying as well as for forward reconnaissance.

But when Gunther Plüschow learned to fly, it was not with thoughts of derring-do aerial battles with enemy pilots. Exploits like those later enjoyed by Manfred von Richthofen, the legendary Red Baron, would not have entered his head. It was just the thought of soaring above the clouds, temporarily unleashed from earth's shackles, that appealed to his free-spirited nature.

16

Again, though, he had to summon up enormous patience. When he arrived at Johannisthal in the new year of 1914, he found the airfield covered in a deep white carpet. For day after day, flying was impossible. Each morning Gunther would wipe the condensation from the windows of his quarters, hoping that the snow would have started to clear, but the temperature remained below freezing and the snow just would not go away. The cold snap lasted for a month and it was the Sunday morning of 1 February 1914 before he could at last sit in the cockpit of the two-seater Rumpler Taube that was to be his training aircraft.

The Taube – the German word for 'dove' – had been initially developed by an Austrian, Igo Etrich, and had first flown in 1910. Licences were issued for serial production by several works including the factory of the Viennese-born Jew, Edmund Rumpler, in Germany. Despite its name, the design had not evolved from the bird but from the dried seed of the Zanonia plant – a large vine of the cucumber family that grows in the dense, moist jungles of Java – which glides to the ground in a slow spin induced by a single wing. Experiments with gliders had eventually produced a powered aircraft and when the bird-like tail and body were added, some people saw the resemblance to a pigeon or dove, and the Taube was born. The aircraft did not possess ailerons (used to control the aircraft in roll) in the wings and the pilot turned the plane by 'warping' the wings using a system of pulleys and cables that twisted the trailing edges of the wings in opposite directions – similar to a bird's wings in flight – and by using elevators at the rear of the tail. The design made for a very stable flight suitable for observation while the aircraft's translucent clear-doped linen covering made it difficult to spot from the ground when it was flying above 1,200ft. The French called it 'the Invisible Aircraft' and some aviation historian historians now regard the Taube as the world's first 'stealth' aircraft. For four years, from 1910 until the end of 1914, when the rapid advancement of aircraft design was rendering it obsolete, the Taube was a hugely popular mono-plane with fifty-four companies, mostly in Germany and

Austria, producing around 500 varieties, each bearing the name of its particular manufacturer.

Just as sailing had come as naturally to Gunther Plüschow as a duck takes to water, so he took to the air as if he were born to fly, or at least to handle an aircraft. The weather was still cold but there was hardly a cloud to be seen and the trainee aviator marvelled at it all as the Taube climbed away from the airfield on his first flight. Plüschow quickly grasped the rudiments of the aircraft, and on the third day his instructor, Werner Wieting, felt confident enough in his young pupil's ability to allow him to fly solo. Two days later, Wieting, already a prominent name in the emerging German aviation industry, asked Plüschow if he would like to attempt the examination. Gunther needed no second bidding, and after a flawless take-off and flight he brought the Rumpler Taube in for a perfect landing. As he clambered out of the machine Wieting was there to greet the newly qualified pilot with a strong handshake. Isot later gave him a medallion bearing the figure '13'. It was to be talisman that he would wear for the rest of his life.

Less than a month after gaining his pilot's insignia, Plüschow was to take part in what he later described as a world record. At the beginning of 1914, Edmund Rumpler had unveiled his Taube 4C. It featured rudimentary ailerons instead of the wing warping of earlier models and its 100hp Mercedes engine gave it a top speed of 75mph, while a 45ft wingspan was designed to help it climb to new heights. Now Rumpler wanted his baby to attempt a new world altitude record. Otto Linnekogel, one of Germany's leading aviators, was chosen to pilot the new version of the Taube and Plüschow was asked to accompany him as observer.

The way Plüschow told the story was that when, after fifteen minutes in the air, they had reached 2,000m (6,560ft) they felt pleased, but thereafter progress was disappointingly slow. The air became bumpy and after an hour they had managed to climb to only 4,000m (13,120ft). Then the engine started to splutter before giving up altogether. They descended in spirals towards the ground, the engine burst back into life, and Linnekogel managed to land the Taube safely. At the greater altitude, the engine had simply frozen.

A few days later, modifications now made to the engine, they tried again. This time they had better luck, climbing steadily to 4,900m (16,072ft). But their fuel had almost run out, the intense cold was again taking its toll on the engine, and they could go no further and returned to the Johannisthal airfield with the German altitude record in the bag, but with the world record still eluding them.

At the beginning of March, the weather improved sufficiently for them to make a third attempt. At 10,000ft they looked out and saw the silver cigar of a Zeppelin airship. Linnekogel flew around the dirigible and they exchanged salutes and waves with its crew. Then they returned to the serious business at hand. After an hour in the air they had attained a height of 4,800m, then 4,900m, and finally the needle on the Taube's altimeter read 5,000m – 16,400ft.

But now the conditions were taking their toll, not on the engine but on the human body. Plüschow suddenly felt drowsy, every movement was an effort, and turning around to look at Linnekogel – the pilot sat behind the observer – was a difficult manoeuvre. Plüschow noticed that the cloud had vanished and that the sky was perfectly clear, so clear that when he looked over towards Berlin he could make out the straight line of the Charlottenburger Chaussee, the broad avenue that led to the Brandenburg Gate, and beyond that the Unter den Linden. Then he looked at his watch and realized that twenty minutes had passed since he had last checked their height. They were still at 5,000m. At that moment Linnekogel signalled that he was returning to the airfield. Plüschow waved at him frantically, spreading out five fingers and pointing upwards. But Linnekogel just laughed, gripped Gunther's hand, shook it hard and then released it, opening and shutting the fingers of his own right hand twice. They were now above Potsdam and all Plüschow had to do was guide them back to a suitable landing place at the airfield.

After one and three-quarter hours in the air, they landed and he was at last able to speak to Otto Linnekogel. It transpired that Plüschow's instruments had frozen at 5,000m but that Linnekogel's, better protected, had continued to function. Apparently they had done it: they had broken the world record by reaching 5,500m (18,040ft). Plüschow wrote later: 'We stood proudly amongst our lesser mortals who had remained on terra firma.'

It is a strange account, to be sure, because in December 1913 the French aviator Georges Legagneux, a serial challenger for the world altitude record, flying a Nieuport Type IIN over St Raphael in France, had achieved 6,120m (20,073ft). The event was widely reported in the newspapers, so quite why Plüschow and Linnekogel thought that they had achieved a world record three months later with a height that was 2,000ft less is difficult to understand. As it turned out, on 9 July 1914 Otto Linnekogel would eventually achieve a new record with a height of 6,600m (21,648ft) over Johannisthal. He held it for only five days, however: on 14 July, another German aviator, Heinrich Oelerich, smashed it by climbing to around 8,000m (26,240ft). In between, Legagneux was killed; he was on a test flight above the Loire at Saumur when the propeller broke as he was attempting a double loop and the aircraft fell into the river. As for Plüschow's claim that he had participated in a world record, the flight no doubt took place as he described, but breaking the record seems to have been a flight of fancy. In fact, two Frenchmen, Roland Garros and Edmond Perreyon, had each achieved a height of more than 5,500m even earlier than Legagneux.

As he awaited details of his journey to Tsingtao, Plüschow asked permission to make a longer overland flight across Germany. Edmund Rumpler agreed to provide an aircraft and by the end of March Gunther had passed his field pilot's course – again, he was awarded this in double-quick time; on average it took about three months to reach this standard, which was much more exacting than simply taking up an aircraft for a spin around an airfield – and was ready for his trip. His observer was

Lieutenant Strehle, a friend who was attached to the War Academy, for whom flying was a new experience. And what an experience it turned out to be.

Their first destination was Hamburg but first Plüschow wanted to give his friend a sightseeing trip. At 1,500ft, he levelled out the Taube to give them a good view of the Havel Lakes. But as they sighted Nauen, 24 miles west of Berlin and home to the world's first radio transmitting station – it had been operational since August 1906 – fog set in. With the confidence that comes with youth rather than experience, Plüschow checked his compass and then flew calmly on into the thick blanket. After about two hours the fog thinned a little and from 2,500ft Gunther peered down and was overjoyed to catch sight of a ploughed field. He brought the Taube in gently and the aircraft bumped across the field until it came to a halt almost in the middle.

It was a local holiday and people from the nearby village were soon hurrying towards them. They helped to pull the Taube over the uneven soil, and cut down some trees to give Plüschow a clear take-off. Then, after accepting the villagers' offers of refreshment – and taking some good-natured leg-pulling – the two military men were back in the skies. Their relief was short-lived. After only fifteen minutes, the fog closed in again. After two hours there was an even more worrying development: the Taube's engine began to act erratically. Plüschow began to check everything and to his horror saw that the needle on his fuel gauge indicated a rapid loss of petrol. He took the Taube down to 2,000ft and saw that they were over the River Alster, the tributary that met the Elbe in Hamburg. Now he needed to find the Fuhlsbüttel airfield to the north of that city.

They were down to their last ten litres of fuel when he saw the setting sun glinting on the airfield's sheds and was able to bring the Taube in on a steep spiral. Only when they had come to a standstill and he could climb out and examine the aircraft did Gunther realize what the problem had been: the lower part of the carburettor was damaged and, with each throb of the engine, petrol had escaped. It was remarkable that there had been no fire.

While they waited for a new carburettor to arrive at Fuhlsbüttel, Plüschow and Strehle spent three days visiting some old friends in Bremen before beginning the next leg of their planned journey – to the Plüschow hometown of Schwerin. The Taube repaired, they took off again, this time not into fog but into a stormy, rain-lashed sky. Plüschow wrote later that it was a journey that he would never again have undertaken in such conditions unless it was in the direst emergency. But, again, the enthusiasm of youth and his lack of experience caught him out. Now fully laden with fuel, all 170 litres, the Taube was at its heaviest and, from the moment of take-off, Plüschow had a fight on his hands to keep the aircraft stable as it was thrown from side to side by strong gusts of wind.

Just 200ft above the Fuhlsbüttel field he saw the first houses of Hamburg in front of him and knew that it would be impossible to gain any more height, or to turn back to the airfield. He saw a small field and decided that that would be their only hope. But as he prepared to land, a fierce gust swept the Taube to one side, tipping it dangerously. The aircraft came down with a jarring bump and Gunther was thrown violently forward, cracking his head on part of the aircraft. The Taube had tilted forward and was standing on its head.

For a few moments there was complete silence and then Plüschow was aware of liquid pouring over his face. Petrol! Somehow, he managed to switch off the engine, despite his being jammed inside the cockpit. Then he called out to Strehle but there was no answer. Gunther knew that his friend, sitting in front of him, must have taken the full impact of the crash.

He called out again and still there was no reply. He feared the worst when at last he heard a voice: 'What happened?'

'Thank God,' said Plüschow. 'Have you broken anything?'

'I'm not sure,' Strehle replied.

Then there were other voices:

'Is anyone in there?'

'Are you still alive?'

'Wait, we'll get you out.'

Their rescuers lifted them clear. Amazingly, Strehle was suffering from nothing more than a strained back. Plüschow had two broken ribs for his trouble. And they had landed in a large manure heap, which had probably cushioned the impact. The two men shrugged off the ignominy of that and thanked their lucky stars.

The Taube would not be flying again, at least not for some considerable time. Edmund Rumpler's reaction is not recorded. Meanwhile, after being patched up at a local hospital, Plüschow and Strehle continued their journey to Schwerin by train, to enjoy several days' holiday walking around the neighbouring countryside and sailing on the many lakes. Schwerin in early spring had much to offer two young military officers looking for some respite from their duties.

Then it was time to leave. For Strehle it was back to the War Academy. For Gunther Plüschow there was a much longer journey, back to one of his former, and much favoured, haunts.

Chapter 4

A Place in the Sun

In November 1897 the brutal murders of Francis Xavier Nies and Richard Henle, two German Roman Catholic priests working for the Steyl Mission in China's southern Shantung province, gave Germany the pretext it needed to occupy Kiaochow, a 200-square mile stretch of the Shantung Peninsula on the Yellow Sea coast that included the port town of Tsingtao.

Germany had been a latecomer in the European race to acquire overseas colonies; as late as 1884 Chancellor Otto von Bismarck had resisted public demands to join in the scramble for Africa. But the clamour proved too strong to ignore and first South-West Africa, then Cameroon, Togo and parts of East Africa found themselves under the German flag, to be followed by territories such as New Guinea, the Marshall Islands and others in the Pacific.

As the fledgling German Empire sought to compete with other Western imperial powers, China became a particular target. Great Britain had acquired Hong Kong as a dependent territory as long ago as 1842, and was about to acquire a lease on Weihaiwei (the British called it Port Edward), in all a 285-square mile territory on the eastern tip of the Shantung Peninsula that would then give the Royal Navy two major Chinese bases. Russia, meanwhile, was putting pressure on China to grant it a lease on Port Arthur (modern-day Lüshun) at the southern end of the Liaotung Peninsula, 272 miles east of Peking. The German government already coveted the deep-water possibilities of Kiaochow but had held back for fear of alienating the Russians. Now the murders of the missionaries presented Germany with the opportunity it wanted.

On 13 November 1897, three warships – the shallow-draft small cruiser *Cormoran*, the light cruiser *Prinzess Wilhelm* and Admiral Otto von Diedrichs's flagship, the heavy cruiser *Kaiser* – arrived off the coast, landed a contingent of 700 marines and, despite some last-minute jitters in Berlin, took possession of the little village of Tsingtao. The protected cruiser *Kaiserin Augusta* sailed from the Mediterranean to join the little fleet and, on 26 January 1898, marines of the III Seebattalion arrived on the Norddeutscher Lloyd passenger liner *Darmstadt* to strengthen the German garrison. By the following March, the Imperial Chinese government had no option but to sign a treaty that leased Tsingtao, a surrounding area of 200 square miles, and the deep-water Kiaochow Bay to Germany for a period of ninety-nine years.

The German plan was to turn Tsingtao into a colony that would function as both a naval base and a trading centre. The so-called 'unequal treaty' allowed them to transform the village into a town, building the official seat of the German governor as well as erecting barracks and private residences, schools and a university, and laying out new streets. Moreover, Germany's new colonies were also serving a greater political purpose. Nationalist lobby groups argued for an even bigger German fleet, the colonies always being described as 'protectorates' to underline their need for permanent military and naval protection.

In December 1897, the State Secretary for the Foreign Office of the German Empire (and a future Chancellor), Bernhard von Bülow, told the Reichstag: 'We must demand that German missionaries, merchants, goods, as well as the German flag and German vessels be treated with the same respect in China that other powers enjoy. In short, we do not want to put anyone in our shadow, but we also demand our place in the sun.'

In Tsingtao, Germany had just that. By March 1904 the harbour there was completed. It included workshops where almost every type of maritime repair could be carried out, and small steamers even built. The 16,000-ton dry dock was the largest in all Asia. Three months later, the 250-mile long railway between Tsingtao and Tsinan-fu, the capital of Shantung province, carried its first passengers. A water works and a sewage treatment plant were fully functional, electrification completed, streets with names like Hamburger Strasse, Kronprinzen Strasse and Prinz Heinrich Strasse were laid out to European designs with trees native to Germany specially shipped in and planted – and churches, schools and a hospital opened their doors. Cafés and beer gardens did ever-increasing business as banks, mining and engineering companies set up offices in Tsingtao as German influence extended to other areas of Shantung province. Merchants traded from their premises in this little bit of Germany in China. A *Warenhause* or department store catered for every shopping need, and in 1903 a brewery began in the German tradition, mainly for Germans and other Westerners; today the Tsingtao Brewery Company still produces world-famous beer.

In theory, many of the businesses in Tsingtao were Sino-German companies. In practice the capital and management were almost always German, particularly the railway and the coalmines that had been opened at Weihsien and Hung-shan. Coal would become an increasingly precious commodity during the changeover from sail to oil-fired warships.

In 1904 the daily *Tsingtauer Neueste Nachrichten* (Latest News of Tsingtao) joined the weekly *Deutsch-asiatische Warte* (German-Asiatic Observer) in the ranks of Kiaochow's German-language press.

As for the general quality of life, Gunther Plüschow's first impressions of Tsingtao when he arrived there on board the *Fürst Bismarck* had been wholly favourable. Tsingtao's climate made it a fashionable summer resort – 'the Brighton – or the Ostend – of the Far East' was the joke among Westerners – and on the Auguste Viktoria Bay, whose bright blue water was dotted with picturesque little islands, junks and sampans, the east beach ran for more than a mile along the Yellow Sea. There were bathing huts and refreshment kiosks, ladies strolled under parasols along its sand, and a long pier jutted out into the sea for further promenading. There were good hotels, too. The Strand Hotel offered a prime location near the beach, and there were also the Central Hotel, the Arnold Bauman Hotel Metropole and the Hotel Prinz Heinrich.

The 'European town', a pretty red-roofed town that had grown up on the southern slope down to the bay, had been built at the expense of Chinese communities that had been demolished to provide a buffer between the Europeans and the 'Chinese town'.

Although much of his service on the China Station had been spent at sea, Plüschow had a special place in his heart for Tsingtao. Going back there really must have seemed like a dream come true. Yet if the good life seemed to be reserved for Germans and their fellow Westerners, by the late 1900s it hid the political reality. Germany's increasing sense of diplomatic isolation, its fear of jeopardizing its commercial interests elsewhere in China and the Chinese insisting on a very narrow interpretation of the terms of the lease, and of the mining and railway concessions, were combining to limit German influence in Shantung. On 1 January 1906, the free port that had previously included the entire Kiaochow protectorate was limited to Tsingtao itself and an adjacent stretch of land. The remaining territory was returned to the jurisdiction of the Chinese customs authority.

By 1913, the year before Plüschow returned, the population of the Kiaochow leased territory was about 200,000, with Tsingtao itself being home to 5,000 Europeans and Japanese, and 55,000 Chinese. They were all administered not by the German Imperial Colonial Office but by the Imperial Naval Office from Government House, an imposing building set amid beautifully laid-out grounds. The governor's mansion, sitting atop a small hill, had been completed in 1907, a strange-looking art nouveau concoction from where Alfred Meyer-Waldeck effectively ruled the protectorate.

A distinguished naval career had seen Meyer-Waldeck serve as chief of staff at Tsingtao and as deputy governor of the Kiaochow leased territory before being appointed governor in 1911. He was a memorable figure – a thick-set man who stood 6ft 5ins tall, had piercing blue eyes and sported a goatee beard – and Gunther Plüschow had met him briefly when the youngster had been serving on the *Fürst Bismarck*, although it is extremely doubtful that a junior officer would have made any impression on the senior man. Now, however, their paths were to cross once more and Tsingtao was to be a most fateful posting for both of them.

Chapter 5

Tsingtao Again

Towards the middle of June 1914, Gunther Plüschow arrived back in Tsingtao, in a China whose political structure was much changed from that of his previous visit. Under Sun Yat-sen's revolution, the Qing dynasty had collapsed, ending 2,000 years of imperial rule. This was now the embryonic Republic of China that had been officially founded in January 1912. Yet Tsingtao itself had changed little from the one that Plüschow remembered from six years earlier. It still retained its dominating European appearance and customs, its status as a German protectorate seeing to that.

Plüschow's journey from Berlin had taken all of fifteen days, quite a portion of its 5,500 miles spent rolling through monotonous steppes and deserts aboard Russia's Trans-Siberian Railway towards Harbin, an important railway administrative centre, and then on to the Manchurian city of Mukden (modern-day Shenyang), a former capital of the Qing dynasty and the site of some of the heaviest fighting of the Russo-Japanese War of 1904–5. Here, Plüschow and his companion, Lieutenant Friedrich Müllerskowski, a fellow aviator of the same age who was to be attached the marines in Tsingtao (Plüschow was to be attached to the cavalry), changed to a Chinese-run train for their onward journey to Peking, Tientsin and then Tsinan-fu, Shantung's provincial capital, where they would change for the final time for the last leg to Tsingtao. At Tapautau, Tsingtao's Chinese quarter to the north, the train stopped to let off the less well-heeled passengers – mostly coolie workers – who had travelled second and third class, and then pulled on slowly to the main 'European' station that stood just over half a mile down the line.

31

Plüschow and Müllerskowski (who had joined the infantry in 1907 and transferred to the Seebattalion in 1912) gathered their immediate belongings and were met by a non-commissioned officer who had organized a horse-drawn carriage to take them to their quarters. As their baggage was loaded on to their transport, Plüschow took stock of the familiar scene in the square outside the station: rickshaws and carts were trundled back and forth, an occasional motor car appeared, carriages did their best to compete, cyclists weaved their way through, and two policemen, one German, the other Chinese, worked hard to control it all. It was a pleasant teatime afternoon and the few European women that were about shaded their Western skin from the late sun.

The German aviators' carriage was pulled by two Mongolian ponies – not really ponies at all but small horses of a breed purported to be unchanged since the time of Genghis Khan – and the animals trotted off eastwards along the shoreline road towards Iltis Platz, Tsingtao's rudimentary racecourse, and soon to be its even more rudimentary military aerodrome.

In fact Tsingtao had seen an aircraft fly even before Plüschow and Müllerskowski arrived. In July 1913, a German businessman called Franz Oster had taken up a Rumpler Taube. Oster had trained as a metalworker before joining the German Navy, which he left at Hong Kong, travelling on to Tsingtao to open a lock-smith's shop, a factory and a small wharf – at one time he was employing 300 Chinese workers – before selling the factory and the wharf to the German government in 1909. Oster returned to Germany, learned to fly, and came back to Tsingtao in 1912, together with his Rumpler Taube. Dissatisfied with its engine, he installed a bigger one and made the first flight over the protectorate on 9 July the following year. When war broke out in August 1914, the governor, Meyer-Waldeck, asked Oster to help with reconnaissance flights but he could not get the aircraft off the ground again and would spend the rest of the war as a prisoner of the Japanese. Gunther Plüschow would obviously have been well aware of Oster but he makes no reference to him in any of his written works. Perhaps this is because Oster was a mere civilian who could not be relied upon to get his aircraft into the sky when it mattered most. None the less, he deserves his place in Tsingtao's story.

When Plüschow and Müllerskowski arrived at Iltis Platz, they found it decorated with flags and bunting, and a football match being played there between teams of German and British sailors. HMS *Minotaur*, the flagship of the Royal Navy's China Station, was paying a goodwill visit to Tsingtao and the East Asia Squadron's commander, Vice-Admiral Graf Maximilian von Spee, was playing host to the British commander, Vice-Admiral Sir Martyn Jerram, aboard his flagship, the armoured cruiser SMS *Scharnhorst* that had replaced the *Fürst Bismarck* in April 1909. The officers exchanged lavish dinners, and the crews competed in various sports events. The football match that Plüschow and Müllerskowski came upon ended in a 1-1 draw but the British narrowly won the overall tournament.

The *Minotaur* was berthed next to the *Scharnhorst* and across from another heavy cruiser, the *Gneisenau*, while the light cruisers *Emden*, *Leipzig* and *Nürnberg*, together with the gunboats *Iltis*, *Jaguar*, *Tiger* and *Luchs*, river gunboats *Tsingtau*, *Vaterland* and *Otter*, and the torpedo boat S-90 made up von Spee's East Asia Squadron. Upon the outbreak of war they would be joined by a new SMS *Cormoran* – the former Russian mail steamer *Rjasan* which ran between Nagasaki and Vladivostok and which was captured by the *Emden*: the guns from the first *Cormoran*, which had suffered engine failure, were transferred to the new ship – and the *Prinz Eitel Friedrich*, the former Norddeutscher Lloyd liner which happened to be at Tsingtao that August and which was also converted to an auxiliary cruiser.

But for now the jollity continued. Von Spee presented a handsome silver cup to the winners of the sports tournament, and the following day Jerram repaid the compliment with a grand ball aboard the *Minotaur* which was all dressed up for the party, with a large striped marquee covering part of a deck. The *Minotaur*'s guns were festooned with Chinese lanterns, the ship's band provided the music, and food and drink was prepared in the galley.

On 12 June, when the *Minotaur* left Tsingtao to resume her duties, Jerram bid farewell to von Spee with the words: 'Live well and goodbye until we meet again.' Sixteen days later, the 19-year-old son of a Bosnian postman shot dead the heir to the Austro-Hungarian throne. There would be no more parties in Tsingtao.

Indeed, the ball aboard the British flagship had been a rare major social occasion on the protectorate: Plüschow later wrote home, complaining that there was no theatre, no music and precious little social life there. There was, however, plenty to be getting on with, not least making his living arrangements as comfortable as possible. The Taubes were still on their way from Germany and were not expected to arrive at Tsingtao until the middle of July, so there was ample opportunity to furnish the house at Iltis Platz that he had chosen to rent, rather than share the officers' quarters. The villa stood high on a hill with a good view of both the airfield and the sea. Behind the house, a good part of it buried deep in the hillside, the huge ferro-concrete Bismarck Barracks that had been built between 1903 and 1909 and which could accommodate up to 4,000 men, overlooked the home that Gunther was to share with a fellow officer, Conrad Patzig, who was aide-de-camp to Tsingtao's divisional commander.

Armed with a book on interior design, Plüschow visited a Chinese cabinetmaker and ordered furniture. He was not the first, nor would he be the last, to marvel at the Chinese capacity for quickly producing cheap and well-executed imitations. Four weeks later, he had everything he wanted and the villa looked perfect. In the meantime, Plüschow decided to invest in some poultry, and when he was not organizing that, he was riding the horse that he had purchased – he called it Fips – and took part in races around Iltis Platz against fellow cavalry officers, played polo and rode out with some of the foreign women who were visiting the summer resort. Suddenly life was picking up, despite the lack of theatre and music. According to Plüschow, Tsingtao was now a 'Paradise on earth', there was horse-riding and tennis to fill the off-duty hours, wonderful beach life where it was possible to meet many interesting foreigners, especially the charming English ladies of the type he remembered so well from his previous visit here. There was one English girl whose company he particularly enjoyed. He wined and dined her, rode out into the countryside with her, went swimming with her, took her for a spin in the motor car that he had acquired. He was, after all, still a single young man, although we must assume that Isot was still central to his long-term plans.

Indeed, Tsingtao was considered a plum posting for any German serviceman. The pleasant climate of mild summers and relatively warm winters, pretty girls, plenty of sport and plenty of good 'German' beer to drink – what could be better? There was even less physical labour than at European postings because at Tsingtao it was Chinese labour, not the rank-and-file sailor of the Imperial German Navy, that did the heavy lifting.

At Iltis Platz, Plüschow had his own Chinese servants to organize, six in all: the houseboys – effectively the officers' batmen – 'Herr Dorsch' and 'Herr Simon' as Gunther called them; Maurice, the cook; Max, who quickly established his reputation as an extremely lazy gardener; Fritz, the perpetually smiling groom who also looked after the chickens; and August, who did the laundry, ran errands and took care of the more menial chores around the villa.

In the middle of July, Gunther Plüschow's life took on a different dimension. The Rumpler Taubes arrived. Together with Müllerskowski he went straight down to the docks and the pair supervised the unloading of the two aircraft on to horse-drawn carts. The Taubes had been disassembled for their long sea journey. The wings and tail section of each plane had been strapped to the fuselage and then crated. There were also two crates of spare parts, one for each aircraft. Unloading the crates

35

containing the aircraft themselves was easy enough at the dock-side, but getting them off at the other end would pose a problem. So it was decided to unpack them as soon as they came off the ship, and then load them on to the carts each of which was pulled by two Mongolian ponies. It was a strange procession that set off for Iltis Platz: the aircraft being trundled along, military policemen marching alongside to keep the large crowd of interested Chinese at bay and Plüschow and Müllerskowski heading the parade on horseback.

To house the Taubes and two static balloons, a hanger had been erected on the racecourse-cum-aerodrome, where a motley crew of sailors, civilian mechanics and Chinese labourers set to work. The Taubes were predecessors of the Type 4C in which Linnekogel and Plüschow had made their world altitude record attempt four months earlier. Both had been delivered to the German Navy late in 1913. Plüschow had been assigned the newer of the two – *E-8*; Müllerskowski was given *E-1*. Work went on round the clock to reassemble the Taubes and on Tuesday, 28 July 1914, Plüschow's was ready to fly.

The airfield was extremely small – 2,000ft long and 650ft wide – and full of obstacles, not to mention being surrounded by hills. Lieutenant Viktor Klobucar, who had passed his pilot's test in 1913 but who was now serving on the Austro-Hungarian Navy's protected cruiser *Kaiserin Elisabeth* that was stationed at Tsingtao, took one look and asked Gunther: 'Do you call this an aerodrome?' According to Klobucar, it looked more like a child's playground and he doubted that anyone could take off or land an aircraft in such a confined space. Gunther Plüschow began to wonder if his friend was right, but there was no other choice. The rest of Tsingtao comprised mostly steep hills, mountains even, and deep ravines. Somehow, he managed to get the Taube into the air and, once there, he put aside thoughts of how he was going to get down again. It was a beautiful, sunny morning and he revelled in the experience of seeing Tsingtao from the air for the first time. But he could not stay in the air forever. As he approached Iltis Platz, the airfield looked even smaller than he remembered and he decided to descend slowly, in wide circles. Eventually the moment arrived and he brought the Taube in. A few moments later he was switching off the engine. The large crowd that had witnessed the flight no doubt shared in his relief. Some noticed the dragon tattoo on his left arm. They called him the 'Dragon Master'.

Among the fascinated spectators was Baron Major General Yasumasa Fukushima, the governor of the Kwantung leased territory that Japan had taken from Russia as a result of the Russo-Japanese War in which he had fought with distinction. Fukushima, from a samurai family, became an officer in the Imperial Japanese Army, seeing service in the Boxer Rebellion in 1900 when he commanded the Japanese forces at Tientsin. He is also thought to have been the founder of the feared Kempeitai, the Japanese Secret Service, but in 1914 he was most famous for his feat of riding non-stop from Berlin to Vladivostok. From 1887 to 1892, Fukushima had served as an attaché in the German capital; after he left he spent one year and four months travelling back alone to Vladivostok, gathering intelligence along the way. On the day of Plüschow's first flight over Tsingtao, Austria-Hungary declared war on Serbia. Two days later, Fukushima decided to leave the protectorate. Officers of the German garrison put on a farewell dinner for him.

The following day it was Friedrich Müllerskowski's turn to take to the air over Tsingtao. Plüschow apparently did his best to warn the marines officer of the various problems that he himself had encountered, not least the difficult air currents on take-off. But Müllerskowski was keen to take some of the glory and perhaps he did not pay sufficient attention to his more experienced colleague, whom he perhaps saw as a competitor. Müllerskowski's Taube was not much more than 150ft into the air when a gust of wind caught the aircraft as it was clearing some trees at the end of the airfield. The plane crashed sideways and was a write-off. Müllerskowski was badly injured. As he did not see active service at Tsingtao, at least not in the face of an enemy, he can hardly be regarded as the first German casualty of the war

37

that was about to erupt. Nevertheless, for the remainder of that war he was held as a POW in Japan, first at the Kumamoto camp and then at Kurume, returning to Germany only in 1919 whereupon he rejoined the army. In 1920 Müllerskowski retired with the rank of major.

Chapter 6
Fighting Talk

Towards the end of July 1914, Gunther Plüschow was looking forward to a polo match against the British Shanghai Polo Club that had been arranged for early August. But in the early hours of 30 July, a private solider arrived at Iltis Platz bringing orders for Plüschow and Patzig to report immediately to divisional headquarters. Even given the enormous political tensions in Europe, they assumed that this was an exercise and, as they pulled on their uniforms, both men grumbled about being awakened at such an unearthly hour. Plüschow was especially annoyed because he had worked late the previous evening. However, when they reported to the divisional commander they discovered that this was no manoeuvre. Events had taken a major turn. They were to go to their duties. Plüschow went straight to the airfield while Patzig made for the 21cm shore battery to which he had been assigned. Over the next few hours neither man had much time to consider events in Europe over the previous month, or indeed those over previous decades, but the denouement was due.

Ever since German unification in 1871 there had been an uneasy balance of power between the great European powers as Germany sought to compete economically and politically. The Germans, by now with the second-most powerful economy after the United States, had long been seen as a threat to the established order and by 1914 it would take only one incident to ignite a chain reaction that would lead to all-out war. On 28 June, in Sarajevo, the capital of the annexed Austrian province of Bosnia, Gavrilo Princip, a member of a nationalist organization seeking Bosnian union with Serbia, shot dead Archduke Franz

Ferdinand, heir to the Austro-Hungarian throne; his wife, Sophie, Duchess of Hohenberg, was also killed. Austria-Hungary's response was over three weeks in coming. On 23 July it issued an ultimatum to Serbia, who it held responsible and with whom it had long-standing differences. The ultimatum was provocative; here, surely, was a chance to end Serbia's challenge to Austro-Hungarian authority in the Balkans. Germany, seeing an opportunity to split the Triple Entente of Britain, France and Russia that surrounded it, and suffocate Russia's modernization into the bargain, endorsed the ultimatum.

Against all expectations, the Serbs' response was surprisingly placatory. But they would not agree to demands that Austro-Hungarian officials be involved in the investigation into the assassinations. That, said the Serbs, would be a direct challenge to their sovereignty.

On 28 July, Austria-Hungary declared war on Serbia. The following day Germany warned Serbia's ally, Russia, not to mobilize. On 30 July, the Russians did mobilize and that was enough to start the telegraph wires humming in Tsingtao and for Gunther Plüschow and the rest of the garrison to be dragged out of their beds in the small hours.

On 31 July, Germany proclaimed *Kriegsgefahrzustand* (threat of war condition) for which the military had been pressing hard since noon the previous day. On 1 August, Germany declared war on Russia, which caused France to mobilize and set in motion the final events that would lead to the First World War. Outside Government House in Tsingtao, people gathered to read the notice that told them that the Kaiser had ordered the mobilization of all army and marine reserves.

German strategy now called for an invasion of Russia's ally, France, and the Schlieffen Plan meant that this would have to be through neutral Belgium. On 2 August, Germany handed Belgium an ultimatum insisting on unfettered passage through that country.

That afternoon Gunther Plüschow was riding through the countryside with his English lady friend. The conversation turned, inevitably, to the political situation and Gunther asked her if she thought that there would be war between their two countries. She told him that, in her opinion, and that of all her friends and acquaintances, the prospect of war between Britain and Germany was quite unthinkable. Gunther agreed. Apart from anything else, he said, such a war would almost certainly mean that the white man's influence in the Far East would be greatly diminished. The Japanese would rush to fill the void. No, war between the two great nations was indeed unthinkable.

But the Belgians flatly rejected the ultimatum they had been given and the following day Germany declared war on France, invading Belgium on 4 August. Now Britain, committed in principle to guaranteeing Belgian neutrality and independence, was dragged into the conflict, whatever the ramifications for her interests overseas. When her ultimatum expired without reply at one hour before midnight on 4 August, she, too, was at war with Germany. In four short weeks, the idyllic life of Tsingtao's garrison, not to mention those of the protectorate's hundreds of civilians of many nationalities, was shattered.

It was also not a good time for the Kaiser's two-Taube airforce in Kiaochow to lose half its strength and, three days after Friedrich Müllerskowski's near-fatal accident, Gunther Plüschow almost came a cropper too. On the Monday morning of 3 August, as Germany declared war on France, Plüschow took off on his first proper reconnaissance flight of the conflict. Japan's intentions were, as yet, unknown, but he was detailed to fly right around the protectorate, looking for anything unusual. He found nothing and was in high spirits as he returned to the airfield at Iltis Platz. He brought the Taube down from 5,000ft to just over 300ft, and was about to make one more circuit before landing at the tight little aerodrome when his engine started knocking, then cut out altogether.

Plüschow could not now reach the airstrip, nor could he manoeuvre the Taube to port or starboard (not that that would have helped much: on the right-hand side of the aircraft was the polo club and a deep ditch; on the left was a hotel and some private villas). Whatever, he could only go straight ahead, towards a small wood. He tried to gain some height but in the thin air the Taube was unresponsive to his yanks on the altitude lever. The Taube skimmed over the treetops and ended up in a ditch, nose down, tail in the air. It had been a close call, especially when the aircraft shot between some telegraph poles and Plüschow, literally, almost lost his head.

The damage to the Taube could have been much worse. The engine was still in one piece, the wings could be mended, and the tangle of wires and canvas could be sorted out. But the propeller was shattered. No matter, back in the hanger, in one of the crates of spares, there were several replacement propellers. But when Plüschow and Franz Stüben, his mechanic, prised open the boxes they were greeted by a terrible sight. In fact, even before they had the lids off, the smell of mould and decay told them that they were in serious trouble. The spare wing-ribs and various wooden parts were covered in some kind of fungus and some of the canvas coverings had rotted. Worst of all, every one of the spare propellers had warped and crumbled. They were all useless.

Undaunted, Plüschow and Stüben, together with two naval stokers, Bruno Frinke and Lorenz Scholl, and eight Chinese labourers from the dockyard, set to work on the rest of the aircraft. One week later, they stood back to admire their work: using what parts were salvageable from the crash and from the crates, they had put the Taube back together again. Except, of course, for its propeller.

It was now time to call upon that particular Chinese skill of producing faithful imitations. Using the least damaged spare propeller as a model, a pattern was made and then seven sections were fashioned from thick oak planks and stuck together using ordinary carpenter's glue. All the work was done by hand and Gunther looked on with a mixture of fascination and dread. Then it was time to put it to the test.

Given the restrictions of the Iltis Platz airfield, it had been a daunting enough task to take off with a perfectly serviceable aircraft. To try it with one that had been partly broken up and then repaired with perishing materials and a makeshift propeller gave Plüschow little confidence that it would not end in disaster. But the Taube did fly, and if the replacement propeller was slower than the original, it still did the job, although on its second flight the layers began to come unstuck and Plüschow managed to land just in time. He initially solved the problem by gluing it back together after each flight but still it kept splitting. Eventually he covered the whole of the leading edges with canvas and sticking plaster to protect the layers from the onrushing air that was forcing them apart. This really was flying by the seat of your pants.

Not only was Gunther the only airman in Kiaochow, and his patched-up Rumpler Taube the only airworthy plane, the protectorate's naval cover was also now desperately thin. The bulk of von Spee's squadron had sailed out of Tsingtao in early July. Of the light cruisers, the *Leipzig* was on her way to change places with the *Nürnberg* which had been off the west coast of Mexico during the Mexican Revolution that had been rumbling on since 1910 and showed no signs of ending. One of von Spee's gunboats sailed towards Hong Kong and the rest of the squadron made for Ponape, a small island in the Carolines. The *Emden* had put to sea on 31 July, the same day that Müllerskowski had written off the other Taube, and she cruised around Korea and Japan before returning to base in heavy seas on 4 August with the *Rjasan* as a prize. Five days later, the new *Cormoran*, the former Russian ship, followed the *Emden* back to sea. She was the last German warship to leave Tsingtao.

The *Emden* – which had left Tsingtao at sunrise with the ship's band playing and the entire crew on deck singing 'Die Wacht am Rhein' (The Watch on the Rhine), Germany's de facto national anthem – rendezvoused with von Spee at Pagan Island in the Northern Marianas chain where all the German ships were taking on large amounts of coal, oil, water and food for a prolonged stay at sea. The squadron suddenly looked quite vulnerable in the hostile Pacific where it was ordered to attack enemy merchant shipping since its chances of breaking through the British blockade and reaching home waters were considered negligible.

'I am quite homeless,' von Spee wrote, 'I must plough the seas of the world, doing as much mischief as I can, until my ammunition is exhausted, or a foe far superior in power succeeds in catching me.'

Eventually, that is what happened. After one moment of glory – victory at the Battle of Coronel on 1 November when HMS *Good Hope* and HMS *Monmouth* were sunk with the loss of 1,600 lives to mark Britain's worst naval defeat of the First World War – von Spee met his own end. Following Coronel, the Royal Navy hunted him down and on 8 December 1914, during the Battle of the Falkland Islands, he went down with the *Scharnhorst*, together with *Gneisenau*, *Nürnberg* and *Leipzig* and some 2,200 German sailors, including von Spee's two sons. The *Emden*'s captain, Karl von Müller, had persuaded the vice-admiral that his ship would be better operating alone and she became the scourge of British shipping in the Indian Ocean. In November 1914, however, after being severely damaged by the Australian cruiser *Sidney*, she was beached in the Cocos Islands. The *Emden* lost 131 men killed and 65 wounded; the surviving members of the crew were taken prisoner and the following year Gunther Plüschow would meet some of them in England. The *Cormoran* had a less distinguished war. Interned at Guam just before Christmas 1914, she was scuttled there by her captain when the United States entered the war in April 1917.

Back in Tsingtao, Meyer-Waldeck had been left with the remnants of the East Asia Squadron: the outdated Iltis Class gunboat *Jaguar*; the minelayer *Lauting* that had been converted from a pleasure steamer; the torpedo boat *S-90*; and four old gunboats. In addition, there was the protected cruiser SMS *Kaiserin Elisabeth*, which had served the Austro-Hungarian Navy since 1890 and which had been at Tsingtao since 22 July 1914. Because of the political situation she had little hope of steaming back to European waters. Eventually, she too was scuttled, but not before she had patrolled alternately with the *Jaguar* and her government had then told most of her crew to abandon her and travel to Tientsin, only to recall them to the ship only an hour after they had arrived there. Such was the already complicated political picture of the war so far as the Far East was concerned.

Against this confusing backdrop, Gunther Plüschow cursed his luck. While the Fatherland was preparing itself for all-out war at home, he was stuck thousands of miles away. The chances that the British or the Russians would attack Tsingtao were remote. The French certainly would not. So he would probably miss seeing action. In the meantime, there was the problem of all those people who had lived and worked alongside the Germans in Kiaochow but who were now enemies. A good example was the relationship between Meyer-Waldeck and the British vice-consul, Reginald Henderson Eckford. They were golfing partners and good friends. But now Eckford was being recalled to London. The two men shook hands and hoped that one day they could resume their friendship. Most of the foreigners began to leave, by train and by ship. The Chinese, too, left in great numbers. Coming the other way were German reservists from all over the Far East. They were a mixed bag, from fit young men to old soldiers who had seen service in different conflicts. Other volunteers turned up: German businessmen keen to do their bit; German merchant sailors who had jumped foreign ships; Germans from the Shanghai Volunteer Corps that had been formed in 1854 to protect foreign settlements from the wars and disorder which plagued Shanghai almost from its earliest days. The volunteers came from British, American, French, German, Russian, Austro-Hungarian, Portuguese, Japanese and other nationalities from all over the world that were living in Shanghai.

45

Some of them were paid regulars, others unpaid part-time soldiers. There were both multinational and national companies. In 1914 the German contingent consisted of one regular and one reserve company. Now many of them made their way to Tsingtao ready to fight for the Fatherland when the call came.

Yet Japan's intentions were still unclear. The country counted itself a major power and with sixteen battleships and fifty-five destroyers it boasted a navy – modelled on the Royal Navy – that was the fourth largest in the world. The Japanese Army – it had had 300,000 men under arms – had been modelled on the Prussian Army, so sympathies were mixed among the ruling elite, many of whom were drawn from the two military services. Japan also had a small but growing industrial base and a colonial empire of sorts, in Taiwan and Korea, as well as interests in China. And it also had a treaty with Britain.

When war between Britain and Germany was declared, the British government, worried about the effect of German cruiser squadrons on its trade in the Pacific, reluctantly asked Japan for help, a request that was apparently quickly withdrawn when the British began to realize the likely consequences of Japan's involvement. But it was too late. Japan, seeing an unprecedented opportunity to eliminate the German base at Tsingtao and effectively turn the Yellow Sea into a Japanese lake, had already agreed and on 15 August 1914 issued an ultimatum to Germany:

> We consider it highly important and necessary in the present situation to take measures to remove the causes of all disturbance of peace in the Far East, and to safeguard general interests as contemplated in the Agreement of Alliance between Japan and Great Britain. In order to secure firm and enduring peace in Eastern Asia, the establishment of which is the aim of the said Agreement, the Imperial Japanese Government sincerely believes it to be its duty to give advice to the Imperial German Government to carry out the following two propositions:

1. Withdraw immediately from Japanese and Chinese waters the German men-o'-war and armed vessels of all kinds, and to disarm at once those which cannot be withdrawn.

2. To deliver on a date not later than 15 September, to the Imperial Japanese authorities, without condition or compensation, the entire leased territory of Kiaochow, with a view to the eventual restoration of the same to China.

The Imperial Japanese Government announces at the same time that in the event of its not receiving, by noon on 23 August, an answer from the Imperial German Government signifying unconditional acceptance of the above advice offered by the Imperial Japanese Government, Japan will be compelled to take such action as it may deem necessary to meet the situation.

The German response was quick and to the point. Meyer-Waldeck issued his own statement that was posted around Tsingtao and also read out at roll call at Bismarck Barracks.

Germany would never surrender Kiaochow to the Japanese or anyone else, said the Governor, who was full of fighting talk. The demand was insulting. For the past seventeen years, hard work and devotion had created a small Germany across the sea. If Japan wanted Tsingtao, then let it try to take it. There would obviously now be an opening of hostilities and it would be a fight to the finish. In a more practical address, Meyer-Waldeck announced plans for an immediate evacuation of women and children. A steamer with accommodation for 600 would leave for Tientsin in a few days, and trains would still be running on the Shantung line.

On Sunday, 23 August 1914, Japan declared war on Germany. Baron Tomosaburo Kato, the Japanese Minister for Foreign Affairs, explained:

47

Early in August the British Government asked the Imperial Government for assistance under the terms of the Anglo–Japanese Alliance. German men-of-war and armed vessels were prowling around the seas of Eastern Asia, menacing our commerce and that of our ally, while Kiaochow was carrying out operations apparently for the purpose of constituting a base for warlike operations in Eastern Asia. Grave anxiety was thus felt for the maintenance of peace in the Far East . . . Therefore, inasmuch as we were asked by our ally for assistance at a time when commerce in Eastern Asia, which Japan and Great Britain regard alike as one of their special interests, is subjected to a constant menace, Japan, who regards that alliance as a guiding principle of her foreign policy, could not but comply to the request to do her . . . While regretting that Japan has been compelled to take up arms against Germany, I am happy to believe that the army and navy of our illustrious sovereign will not fail to show the same loyalty and valour which distinguished them in the past, so that all may be blessed by early restoration of peace.

Four days later, in the early dawn of 27 August, a naval gunner from Munich called Jakob Neumaier was on lookout at the battery on Iltis Hill when he saw a number of black shapes on the eastern horizon. From his balcony at Iltis Platz, Gunther Plüschow was also looking out across the deep blue bay, thinking what a wonderful sight it was. Then he too noticed the shapes. He raised his telescope and saw a number of torpedo boat destroyers of the Imperial Japanese Navy gathering at the entrance to Kiaochow Bay. He called Patzig and then made his way to the airfield. There was work to be done.

Chapter 7

War Footing

Defensive preparations of sorts had been under way in Kiaochow well before Japan's declaration of hostilities. The violent anti-foreigner, anti-Christian Boxer Uprising had led Germany to fortify its important naval and trading base at Tsingtao as far back as 1900. The rugged mountains that stretched along the border formed the protectorate's natural outer barrier, climbing as high as 1,300ft and with few passes to aid an invading force. A second defensive line was formed by the steep hills that ran for 10 miles from Prinz Heinrich Hill to Kuschan. The innermost defensive line lay along the hills that rose between 250ft to 650ft from Iltis to Bismarck to Moltke and overlooked Tsingtao itself. Against a well-equipped, highly trained foe, Germany would need a full infantry corps to hold the outer line; even the second line would require a division. And as at the beginning of the twentieth century the only invaders were likely to be poorly armed, undisciplined Chinese guerrilla fighters, von Tirpitz, the Navy Secretary, saw little point in diverting money from his battle fleet to spend on ground troops. By the time Japan threatened in 1914, it was too late to move such huge numbers of infantry into Kiaochow, so the Germans strengthened their defences along the innermost line.

Tsingtao was still overwhelmingly a naval town. Its seaward defences comprised four gun batteries – in Tsingtao city itself, inland at Bismarck Fort, Hsiauniwa Fort on the south side of the harbour, and Hweichuen Fort which was on a point just less than a mile south of the Iltis Platz airfield and which Gunther Plüschow used as a navigation marker – together with search-lights and about 300 naval mines.

The land defences centred on five large redoubts built between 1909 and 1913. Each was self-sufficient with its own kitchen, bakery, power generator, ammunition magazine and sleeping accommodation for some 200 men. The redoubts were protected by trenches and reinforced concrete dugouts, searchlights and barbed wire, and by two hill batteries, at Iltis Hill and at Moltke Hill, as well as by twelve open gun-pits. Land mines – some hastily fashioned out of small-calibre naval shells – and naval mines were laid and fields of fire cleared, which meant the chopping down of many of the trees so loved by the inhabitants of peacetime Tsingtao.

About 750 naval gunners manned Tsingtao's batteries, while 1,300 marines of the III Seebattalion comprised four infantry companies, a cavalry company (which the Chinese called the Mountain Navy Horsemen), a field artillery battery, an engineering company and two horse-drawn machine-gun companies. Reservists, including members of the East Asiatic Naval Detachment based in Tientsin and Peking, added about 1,500 men, many of them taking up signalling and logistics posts or manning guns. Taking into account sailors who were landed from ships, the total Tsingtao garrison numbered about 4,000 personnel. Around 100 Chinese policemen, dressed in khaki Chinese-style uniforms with blue puttees, maintained internal order.

The Governor's senior officers included Captain Ludwig Saxer, the 45-year-old Tsingtao Chief of Staff, and Captain Waldemar Vollerthun, who was visiting Kiaochow when war was declared and who was now in charge of the protectorate's communications. The III Seebattalion's Lieutenant Colonel Friedrich von Kessinger, an unpopular disciplinarian from Dresden who possessed piercing eyes, commanded the German land forces. Captain Ernst Soldan commanded the engineers. Lieutenant Colonel Paul Kuhlo was in charge of the men that had reported from Peking and Tientsin. Major Edward Kleeman commanded the 5th Company of the III Seebattalion. Major Georg von Kayser was the interpreter.

Meyer-Waldeck moved his headquarters to the Bismarck Fort and waited to see what the Japanese would do. Would they attack? Or would they lay siege? The German garrison had plenty of food but the annual resupply of ammunition had been due that September, although the garrison did have access to the cruiser squadron's reserves. Whatever the Japanese strategy would be, if the Germans could hold Tsingtao until victory in Europe was achieved – and like the optimistic British, most Germans thought that the war would be won by Christmas – then the danger to the Kiaochow protectorate would probably be over too. A couple of Meyer-Waldeck's senior officers even wanted to go so far as to launch an attack on the British war anchorage at Weihaiwei. The Governor wisely squashed the idea flat.

While Tsingtao waited, wild rumours began to circulate: after a decisive victory over the Royal Navy, the German fleet was on its way; a Chinese warlord had raised 80,000 troops who were at this very moment en route to Kiaochow to wipe out the Japanese force; in fact, according to some, the United States had forbidden Japan to attack Tsingtao anyway, so there was no need to worry. And as always in wartime, there were plenty of spy scares.

The German military staff ignored the rumours and concentrated their minds on the likely scenarios. It would be all but impossible for a large force to make it to Kiaochow over the dreadful roads that connected one small walled Chinese village to the next. Landing a small force near Tsingtao itself would not be a viable option because, even if it successfully overcame the heavily mined beaches, it would find itself cut off from the main Japanese force.

As various Japanese options were discussed, Gunther Plüschow made several reconnaissance flights. He did so without an observer because he dared not risk overloading the patched-up Taube. There was still opposition to the use of the aircraft; several German officers felt that it was no more than a toy that got in the way of real soldiering. One afternoon Plüschow flew over the south coast of the Shantung Peninsula, looking as usual

51

for approaching enemy ships, or for troops being landed. There was nothing. He wrote out his report and then went up to Government House to see a colleague. Plüschow tells how he bumped into a senior officer who had rushed out of a conference to pick up some papers. The officer was hurrying back to his meeting when he saw Plüschow and called out to him: 'Have you been flying again today?'

'Yes sir,' replied Plüschow.

'Any sign of the enemy?'

'No sir. Just the warships beyond the Hay Rocks.' (Two uninhabited small islands some 18 miles from Tsingtao were known as Big Hay Rock and Little Hay Rock; the Japanese fleet had been lying there for days.)

According to Plüschow the officer looked astounded. A reconnaissance party had reported that a large Japanese convoy had been sighted steaming towards the coast. The aviator was rushed into the conference to confirm that the report had been a complete invention. Suddenly Plüschow felt that his role in the forthcoming conflict would now prove to be a vital one.

Chapter 8

Under Siege

The Japanese had chosen Lieutenant-General Mitsuomi Kamio to oversee the attack on Tsingtao. Kamio had distinguished himself in the Russo-Japanese War and enjoyed a reputation for solid caution rather than brilliant tactical soldiering. He was a great believer in careful planning and the use of logistics and overwhelming firepower to minimize Japanese casualties. As Meyer-Waldeck had already surmised, that approach ruled out a beach landing near Tsingtao, where the German defenders could counter-attack and catch an exposed Japanese force before it had time to establish a foothold. Instead, Kamio decided to land at Lungkow in neutral China, about 180 miles north of Kiaochow Bay on the opposite side of the peninsula. The Japanese, who desperately wanted to challenge Germany's trade supremacy in the region, had long coveted Lungkow. Indeed, when in December 1913 the Chinese opened Lungkow, for centuries an insignificant junk port, to international trade, it did so entirely at Japan's behest.

Kamio's plan was to land a division first, then bring ashore his siege artillery. However, the campaign had already opened, not on land but at sea. On 22 August, the day before the expiration of the Japanese ultimatum, the torpedo boat *S-90* was covering the *Lauting* as she sowed mines 12 miles from Tsingtao when three Royal Navy warships came into sight. One of them, the River (E) Class torpedo boat destroyer HMS *Kennet*, attacked *S-90*, whose commander, Helmut Brunner, ordered his vessel to steam towards the *Lauting* to warn her. The larger, faster *Kennet*'s first three shots did no more than deluge *S-90* with water, and Brunner ordered his gun crew to return fire. As the

S-90's engineers delivered an astonishing 22 knots, the German boat scored a direct hit on the *Kennet*'s bridge and then put one of her guns out of action. None the less, the British ship continued her pursuit, her captain, the splendidly named Lieutenant Commander Frederic Archibald Hunter Russel, reckoning that he could cut *S-90* off from the harbour entrance. And that he could have achieved had he taken the west side of a small island, but it was badly charted, marked 'shallow', and he thought it might be mined and so took the same course as *S-90* which sped round to the east, just making it back to harbour closely followed by the *Lauting*. Then a 240mm shell fired from the Hweichuen Fort battery sent up a huge plume of water close to the *Kennet* which disengaged. The British destroyers vanished from sight. The *Kennet* had suffered three dead and six wounded, including Hunter Russel. There were no German casualties.

Watching all this from the balcony of his villa was Gunther Plüschow, who had just come off duty. Indeed, the whole garrison, including Meyer-Waldeck, was taking in the spectacle. It was a small but morale-boosting victory for the Imperial German Navy.

Five days later, Vice-Admiral Sadakichi Kato, his flag in the *Suwo*, one of eight Russian pre-dreadnought battleships captured by the Imperial Japanese Navy during the Russo-Japanese War, began blockading Tsingtao with his Second Fleet. British naval intelligence felt that the bulk of von Spee's East Asia Squadron had already fled, but Kato's force of old battleships and cruisers was reinforced by two dreadnoughts, a battle cruiser and two new pre-dreadnought battleships. Seizing several small coastal islands as observation posts – the first occupation of German territory in the First World War – the Japanese began minesweeping.

One of Tsingtao's great attractions was its climate, which not only provided a wonderful posting for German servicemen but more importantly also offered a safe haven to shipping for most of the year. In particular, the Shantung Peninsula usually boasted mild, dry autumns. However, the area was not without its occasional climatic disasters and in the nineteenth century devastating floods had resulted in substantial emigration from the region; in 1914 the whole peninsula would be soaked as the typhoon rains that had normally passed by late summer continued unabated. In early September, the weather claimed the first ship to be lost in the Tsingtao campaign when the Japanese Asakaze Class destroyer *Shirotaye* ran aground on Lientau Inlet, south of Tsingtao. The crew escaped but *Jaguar*, guarded by coastal batteries, came out of harbour and destroyed the *Shirotaye*.

It was the weather that also disrupted Mitsuomi Kamio's plans for a landing at the harbour at Lungkow. On the night of 2 September, four infantry companies and a machine-gun company were rowed ashore. Inside twenty-four hours the engineering battalion that followed them had built a floating pier and two stone quays, allowing a cavalry squadron and an infantry regiment to begin coming ashore. In all, Kamio had more than 20,000 men under his command at Lungkow – and soon a chaotic, nightmarish scene confronted all of them.

Torrential rain, which eventually lasted for ten days, had flooded the beach. Troops hauled their feet out of the mud and struggled on, distressed mules fell to the ground as the carts they were pulling became stuck fast in the mud, and weary soldiers watched as the crates of equipment that they had just unloaded began to float back out to sea. The noise was indescribable as wind and rain lashed those battling to get ashore and those already there. A small brook, over which Japanese engineers had just constructed a pontoon bridge, rose 6ft in less than an hour, sweeping the bridge away. Whole villages were destroyed by flash floods as thousands of Chinese peasants were killed in one of Shantung's worst natural disasters in living memory. Three soldiers were the first German casualties of the Tsingtao campaign; out on reconnaissance, they were drowned as they attempted to cross the swollen Litsun River.

While Kamio's forces fought the elements, China protested at the Japanese invasion of its soil but could do nothing to oppose it. Instead, on 3 September the Chinese announced an area of qualified neutrality 'at such points within Lungkow, Laichow, and the neighbourhood of Kiaochow Bay adjoining thereto as are absolutely necessary for the passage and use of belligerent troops'. Thus, although Japan had violated Chinese territory, China quickly delimited the war zone:

> Within this war zone, our Government will not be wholly responsible as a neutral state; while in all other places within our territory, the Law of Neutrality which has already been promulgated shall remain in force.

In other words, it was too late to argue so the easiest thing to do was to temporarily redraw the map and avoid a conflict.

Untroubled by the politics of it all, Kamio had been forced to call a halt to the landings at Lungkow and ordered those troops who had managed to get ashore to move inland as quickly as possible, although it was slow going. Five days later, a break in the bad weather allowed the cavalry to begin advancing, followed by the infantry. It was impossible for supply columns to follow them because most of the primitive roads in Shantung's interior had been washed away, so the invaders had to supplement half-rations by living off the land or taking advantage of what food they could find in local markets that had escaped the worst of the storm. It was a wet, miserable, bedraggled army that struggled forward. A British report later summed up the dreadful conditions:

> the loose soil is washed away, the sides of the nullahs [ravines or gullies] fall in, carrying with them shelter for the troops; every valley becomes a torrent and every road or track a mass of deep mud . . . Cover for the men, both from fire and the weather, becomes impossible. The men have been soaked through for as much as forty-eight hours and

equipment has been buried by falls of earth . . . ammunition
has rusted . . .

~

In Tsingtao itself there had been excitement – and concern – of
a different kind when a Japanese seaplane flew overhead. The
observer reported that most of the German East Asia Squadron
had indeed escaped and so Japanese sea power was reorganized.
Kato released the extra ships that had been attached to his own
fleet and they now joined others of the Japanese Imperial Navy in
searching out von Spee's ships. In the meantime, the Royal Navy
provided Kato with HMS *Triumph*, a Swiftsure Class pre-
dreadnought battleship that had been ordered by Chile. When
the Chileans put her up for sale in 1903, Britain had bought her
to prevent her becoming part of the Russian fleet. She had been
in reserve at Hong Kong when the war started and was recom-
missioned there. The *Triumph*, which had a noticeably foreign
appearance, with taller, narrower funnels than standard on
British battleships and a pair of heavy cranes amidships, would
be heavily involved in the siege of Tsingtao.

Britain also supplied ground troops, not least because they
were concerned at the willingness with which Japan was apparently prepared to fight in Shantung and soon realized that they
needed to maintain a presence there. On 20 September, Brigadier
General Nathaniel Barnardiston, commander of the Tsingtao
Expeditionary Force, put ashore at Laoshan harbour on the east
coast, just within the leased territory. His force comprised 1,000
men of the 2nd Battalion, South Wales Borderers, commanded
by Lieutenant Colonel Hugh Casson, and supporting staff from
the Army Service Corps and the Royal Army Medical Corps.
They were followed on 22 October by a half-battalion of the 36th
Sikhs, 500 men under the command of Lieutenant Colonel
Edward Sullivan. The Borderers were still in tropical uniforms
that drew astonished looks from Japanese soldiers who wondered

why the British had turned up wearing shorts. However they were dressed, Japan did not want the British there and insisted that they remained subordinate to them. Barnardiston would soon have his differences with the Japanese overall commander.

Before the British arrived, the Japanese had already scored some successes. On 13 September, Japanese cavalry came across a German outpost near the walled town of Tsimo, 25 miles from Tsingtao and just outside the Kiaochow territory. After a brief engagement, the Germans fled. The next day the Japanese took control of an area that cut the Shantung railway which was largely unusable anyway because it had suffered damage by both sides in the early stages of the conflict.

A week earlier, on the morning of Sunday, 6 September, Gunther Plüschow had experienced his first taste of enemy fire. He was flying far out over Kiaochow when he spotted a Japanese column – infantry, cavalry, artillery and supply wagons – struggling along a muddy road near Pingtu, over 60 miles from Tsingtao. His appearance above them was greeted with rifle and machine gun fire. Plüschow's role, of course, was one of observer not fighter pilot – such a creature did not exist – and he turned for home. After landing at Iltis Platz he examined the Taube and found ten bullet holes in various parts of the aircraft. Thereafter, in order to minimize the chances of damage to the engine or to the makeshift propeller, he resolved not to fly so low.

It was his second hair-raising airborne escapade of this short war, although on the previous occasion it had involved, not the Taube, but a balloon. When he was in Berlin awaiting his travel details for the move to Tsingtao, Gunther had been on a course for pilots of dirigibles and for those handling balloons. At Iltis Platz there was a new eight-man section that consisted of two balloons – a kite balloon for observation and a meteorological balloon – together with maintenance equipment and even the means to produce gas. Besides Plüschow, the only man in the protectorate who knew anything about such matters was a petty officer who had some experience of working with airships.

Together they unpacked the balloons and filled them. When the yellow cigar-shaped observation balloon (Second World War barrage balloons were modelled on them) rose into the air and tugged at its moorings, the men exchanged satisfied looks. Then they hauled it down and Plüschow stepped into the tiny wicker gondola. But they had brought it down by its rope rather than by winching the steel cable. When the rope was released, it was measured out too generously and the balloon shot up violently before jerking to a halt, almost tipping Gunther out of the gondola that was now 150ft from the ground. Luckily, he was able to hang on, the steel mooring cable held firm and the balloon steadied.

Meyer-Waldeck had great hopes that the balloon would be invaluable in observing Japanese troop movements but, apart from the obvious dangers to the observer, Plüschow was not at all sure. As far as he was concerned, the Taube was the only effective means of aerial reconnaissance. So it proved when the kite balloon was allowed to reach its maximum height and it was still not possible to see the enemy's movements behind the chain of mountains that formed a semi-circle behind Tsingtao, which was otherwise surrounded on three sides by the sea. There was also another, later, incident when Japanese fire directed at the kite balloon so rattled its observer that he refused to go up again. To prove his point, when the meteorological balloon was hoisted as a decoy the next day, enemy fire destroyed it.

The weather closed in again and, as the Japanese now had the upper hand in the north, Kamio decided to abandon the bridgehead at Lungkow. The troops already ashore – cavalry, engineers and the 23rd Infantry Brigade – would make for Tsimo to set up headquarters there, while the 24th Infantry Brigade would re-embark and make for Laoshan Bay. The plan was simple:

Tsingtao would be cut off from the rest of Kiaochow by Japanese troops on land, and from the rest of the world by the blockading fleet at sea.

On 14 September, Japanese torpedo boats raided Shatzikou Bay to the east of Laoshan harbour, shelling German positions there for several hours. Plüschow had motored up to the area to survey the advanced outposts. As he pulled up, he saw that the soldiers based there were all lying on the ground. Then he realized why. Not a dozen feet away a shell hit a house. Plüschow leapt from his car and joined the others taking cover. They spent the next two hours sheltering from the barrage. Eventually, the Japanese left and the Germans could investigate the damage. The house had been hit, but the damage was not as bad as they had feared. Chinese servants were already collecting shrapnel for souvenirs and three of them raced up to the German officers, each placing down an unexploded shell. The Chinese looked quite proud. The Germans went pale and the shells were quickly removed to a safe place.

Plüschow now confirmed reports from Chinese scouts that enemy warships had been sighted steaming towards the northeast coast of the peninsula. Just before dawn on 18 September, Japanese cruisers bombarded the empty beaches at Laoshan, and then infantry started landing north of the bay, at Wang-ko Chuang, still in Chinese territory. That evening, an infantry company seized the mountainous Hotung pass, 5 miles from the landing ground. A German outpost of forty men under the command of Hans Below, a teacher in Tsingtao and a reserve lieutenant in the marines, withdrew after a lengthy firefight. With the pass secured, the Japanese now enjoyed an unimpeded passage into Kiaochow itself.

Kamio's force also enjoyed total air supremacy. The Navy Flying Corps boasted four seaplanes, French-built Maurice Farman biplanes that were each equipped with six to ten bombs improvised from artillery shells weighing up to 45lbs that were released through metal tubes on each side of the cockpit. They operated from Japan's first aircraft carrier (and the first in the world to be used anywhere in combat), the *Wakamiya Maru* that had been converted from a transport ship that itself had been adapted from a Russian freighter captured in 1905 on its way from Cardiff to Vladivostok. The seaplanes were lowered by derrick on to the water, from where they took off, and then retrieved from the water once their mission was completed. One – flown by Lieutenant Hideho Wada – was a three-seater and had a top speed of 62mph and a ceiling of 9,800ft; it was later fitted with a machine gun. The others, two-seaters, each had only 75hp engines with a top speed of 52mph and a much lower ceiling, so Lieutenant Wada's aircraft did most of the work until another 100hp machine arrived from Japan.

The Farmans joined the Japanese fleet on 1 September and four days later Wada dropped several bombs over the Bismarck battery. They all landed harmlessly in the mud. It was a disappointing start to the history of aerial bombardment for this was the first time that bombs of such size, and designed to be aerodynamic, had been dropped on an enemy. Six days earlier, a German Taube had dropped a few 7lbs explosive devices on the outskirts of Paris; and three years earlier, on 1 November 1911, the Italian pilot Giulio Gavotti had lobbed four 1lb hand grenades out of an Etrich Taube while flying over Ottoman troops in Libya. In 1913, an American soldier of fortune, Leonard Bonney, flying a Moisant pusher biplane for the Mexican government, had dropped small bombs with shotgun shell detonators developed by Mexican mining engineers during that country's civil war. Bonney aimed the Moisant at his target, dropping the bombs just before he pulled out of his dive. So he is credited with inventing dive-bombing, but it is to Hideho Wada that we have to credit the first 'proper' bombing in conflict. The Farmans' main value, of course, was the same as that of Gunter Plüschow's Taube: observation.

The *Wakamiya Maru* eventually struck a mine in the entrance of Laoshan harbour and had to be beached to prevent her sinking. Her engines were disabled owing to steam pipes breaking, her No. 3 hold was flooded, and one man was killed. The Farmans were transferred to a beach airstrip at Shatzikou Bay. The Japanese Army also built an airstrip near Tsimo, thirty minutes' flying time from Tsingtao, from where they flew four Farmans equipped with wheels not floats, and a French Nieuport NG2 monoplane, although that was rarely reported to be in the air.

In the coming weeks, Plüschow would have several uncomfortable meetings with both sets of aircraft. The seaplanes in particular enjoyed a considerable advantage over the Taube: they could operate from a greater distance, take off from a variety of positions, and their ceiling put them out of range of German artillery. A main Japanese objective was to destroy the Taube, and to this end they shelled and bombed Iltis Platz frequently. Although many devices failed to explode, several Chinese were wounded both by explosions and bullets. Plüschow had his small group construct, from planks sailing canvas and tins, a dummy aircraft while the real one lay hidden in the reinforced hanger at the edge of the airfield. Later, he related how one Farman hit the imitation Taube as he sat with the proper one in the hanger. Then he wrote a cheeky note on a shell splinter and dropped that over the enemy's seaplane station.

It was not the only item that he dropped on the Japanese. Engineers had prepared makeshift bombs, filling 4lb tin boxes, used for storing coffee, with sticks of dynamite, nails and bits of scrap metal. A lead spar was fixed to the bottom and a fuse at the top. The contraption exploded when a sharp iron point hit the percussion cap of a cartridge. Their effect was minimal: when he scored a direct hit on a torpedo boat, the bomb failed to go off; another bounced harmlessly off the roof of a British mess tent; he aimed two bombs at the repair ship *Kwanto Maru* that had come to examine the damaged *Wakamiya Maru* in Laoshan harbour and succeeded only in soaking some of her crew; several times he missed hitting a convoy. There might have been one success.

Sometime later someone told him that a bomb he had dropped on a marching column had killed thirty Japanese soldiers.

If it was at all possible, Plüschow avoided the Farmans. His reconnaissance role was far too important to risk being shot down. But he did claim that he had himself shot down one enemy plane after firing thirty shots at it from a 9mm Luger pistol. The details are scant and it seems extraordinary, given that he was a lone pilot in a slower, unwieldy aircraft facing a relatively well-armed aircraft that had two or even three crew. Plüschow's claim that he was probably the first airman ever to shoot down another aeroplane was certainly unsubstantiated, unlike that of the French pilot Sergeant Joseph Frantz, flying a Voisin LA 'chicken coop' with his observer, Corporal Louis Quénault. On 5 October 1914 they definitely shot down a German two-seater Aviatik B1 over the Western Front. Witnessed by French troops on the ground, it thus became the first confirmed air-to-air combat victory. Plüschow made no official report of his incident, although it must be remembered that he was disobeying orders in engaging the enemy; and according to Robert E Whittaker in his book, *Dragon Master*, there is one Japanese airman, Lieutenant Shigematsu, listed as killed in action while flying a Maurice Farman in 1914. No other details are available so the mystery remains, tantalizingly, just that.

On one occasion, Plüschow almost met his own end. Flying at about 5,000ft over the Japanese seaplane station, he saw a Farman taking off. About forty minutes later he saw the biplane closing on him and it was a close-run thing before he made it to Iltis Platz and landed safely.

Landing at the airfield, difficult enough in peacetime, took on an entirely different aspect now that enemy gunners had his range. Plüschow always came in over the city from the sea, but he varied his style, sometimes coming down at speed in wide circles, once even suddenly shutting off his engine and gliding in at a steep angle to kid the Japanese that they had hit him before he levelled out at the last minute. Whichever way he chose, it was always to the accompaniment of shrapnel bursting around him.

And because he dared not risk carrying a passenger, he had to make all the observation notes himself. First he would throttle the engine so that the aircraft would maintain the same altitude for a few moments, then he would snatch a quick look at the enemy's positions and, steering the Taube with his feet, scribble the details down in his notebook. So practised did he become, he said, that he was soon able to do this for an hour or more.

He also had to be inventive. Because of the makeshift propeller, the Taube had difficulty in reaching a decent take-off speed, so Plüschow had a rope attached to the aircraft's tail and three of the largest ground crew he could find then clung on until the Taube was straining at the leash, tugging the men down the field. Upon the pilot's hand signal, they let go together and the aircraft, which had now gathered enough momentum, climbed away. When it came to landing on the increasingly pock-marked strip, the Taube did not have the luxury of the claw braking device of later models which bit into the ground when operated by the pilot. So at the end of the runway Gunther planted two bamboo poles, to each of which was attached a rope. On the ends of the rope were two sandbags. As he landed, his ground crew lifted the rope to catch the runner under the aircraft's tail, slowing it down to a standstill. There was more danger to face than just enemy aircraft.

And besides being a threat to the pilot of the Taube, the Farmans were also of considerable concern to the civilian population. Anti-aircraft guns were built from artillery taken from the *Kaiserin Elisabeth*, and an air-raid warning system was set up. On the 330ft-high Signal Hill, to the south-west of Bismarck Fort, a tall pole was erected: one red ball for an aircraft in sight; two black balls for an aircraft overhead when everyone except essential personnel had to take shelter. Most people did not wait for the black ones.

On the ground Meyer-Waldeck had decided to take the fight to the enemy. On the day that the British expeditionary force began landing at Laoshan Bay, the Governor ordered a counter-attack against a Japanese position on the Kletter Pass, high up in the Laoshan mountains near Tsimo. Under the command of 46-year-old Major Ernst Anders, a German force of 130 men with rifles, four machine guns and two field guns surprised the outpost. There was a furious two-hour firefight – amazingly, each side suffered only two wounded – before Japanese reinforcements arrived and the Germans withdrew. But they had given the enemy a bloody nose.

On 26 September, his force now firmly established, Kamio ordered a general advance. Many of the Germans' scattered mountain outposts fell quickly although *Kaiserin Elisabeth*, *S-90* and *Jaguar* bombarded the Japanese right, destroying an observation post and silencing a field battery that had engaged them.

None the less, the advance continued apace and Meyer-Waldeck knew that he would soon have to abandon the second line as well. But he still had Prinz Heinrich Hill which offered excellent observation for miles in all directions as well as being difficult for an attacking force to climb. Even when the rest of the second line fell, an outpost on Prinz Heinrich Hill could direct fire on to the enemy rear. Plüschow had pointed this out after one of his survey flights, and German signallers quickly erected a telephone and heliograph that kept the observers – who were given enough provisions to last them for two months – in touch with land batteries within the innermost defensive line.

Other means of communication included wireless contact with the Shanghai-based *Sikiang*, a small steamer of the Hamburg-Amerika Line that relayed world news to the beleaguered protectorate, various telephone links and three portable two-way radio sets, together with equipment from an earlier age, including heliograph mirrors and semaphore. There was even a carrier pigeon post at Cape Jaeschke which stood at the mouth of Kiaochow Bay, 8 miles from Tsingtao city, and which was named after a former governor. Here in a deserted police station Lieutenant Bruno Cordua and his two men set up shop with fifteen pigeons, signal lamps and food, including a good supply of birdseed.

At the end of September, the Imperial Japanese War Department issued a press release that was later reproduced in the magazine *Flight*:

> One monoplane and two biplanes of our Aviation Corps left their base of operations between 6.50 and 7 o'clock in the morning of the 27th and bombed the enemy's vessels to the west of Tsingtao. They threw many bombs from an altitude of from 700m to 800m. According to the observations of the aviators, most of the missiles either effectively hit the enemy's vessels or exploded close to them. The enemy were thrown into great confusion, and consequently moved to and fro to dodge the bombs and fired their quick-firing rifles and machine guns promiscuously. One of our biplanes was hit by a machine gun bullet, the other by twenty-six bullets and two gun shots and the monoplane by five bullets. None of the crews or motors, however, were hurt . . .

In the interests of propaganda, morale, call it what you will, there was an obvious spin on the Japanese communiqué. However, German communications themselves would soon suffer another serious blow. On the night of 27–28 September – in appalling weather conditions – a company from Japan's 46th Infantry Regiment, supported by an engineering platoon, attacked the observation post at Prinz Heinrich Hill. Probably due to the rain and wind that lashed the hill, they managed to reach the post without its occupants hearing them. It had been a heroic effort, climbing up in the dark, cutting steps and using ropes, and as dawn broke the main force – an infantry platoon had been detached to try another route – surprised the Germans who nevertheless pinned down their attackers on the lip of the hill. For three hours the main force came under withering fire, its commander and second-in-command both being killed. Then help arrived in the form of the detached platoon which had actually got itself lost before appearing on the other side of the post. Caught in enemy crossfire, the German commander raised a white flag and said he would surrender if the Japanese allowed him and his men to return to Tsingtao. They were having none of it and forty Germans were taken prisoner (a handful of others had managed to escape) and the observation post seized at the cost of twenty-four Japanese killed. Japanese engineers now constructed their own camouflaged observation post. It looked out over all Tsingtao. It was the turning point of the siege.

Meyer-Waldeck was shaken by the loss of the Prinz Heinrich Hill post. Not only that, the second line was now undergoing a huge naval bombardment. As the garrison fell back to the inner line, *Kaiserin Elisabeth*, *Jaguar* and *S-90*, who were supporting the withdrawal, were all hit by fire from land batteries. As the ships withdrew, Kamio brought his troops right up the inner defences and at the same time gave the order for Shatzikou Bay, which had long been evacuated by the Germans, to give him a base much closer to Tsingtao. After two minesweepers had cleared the bay itself, engineers built a pier, a road, and even a narrow-gauge railway for bringing up shells, as well as laying concrete platforms for heavy artillery.

As the Japanese moved ever closer to Tsingtao's final line of defence, heavy German land batteries began shelling the attackers' rear in the hope of disrupting their progress. In his Taube, Plüschow directed their fire as best he was could, but he was outnumbered nine to one by the Farmans and had little time to correct the fire of wayward batteries. In their ignorance, the defenders felt that their bombardment was so heavy that they must be seriously hampering Japanese preparations for a final advance. The loss of their network of Chinese mercenary scouts – some would call them spies – made them no wiser and on the night of 2 October, the Germans launched a raid on the enemy's right flank. One company found only empty trenches; two others drew fire and lost twenty-nine men killed and six captured.

Meyer-Waldeck now knew that the German bombardment had failed to stem the progress of the Allies, who were digging in about a mile from the inner defensive line. Kamio's tactics were for a textbook siege: S-shaped trenches, parallels and saps (covered trenches or tunnels dug to a point near or within an enemy position). We can now call the attacking force the Allies because the British contingent had caught up with the Japanese and it was now something of a joint operation, albeit one firmly in Japan's hands, something that irritated the British commander.

There were already inevitable differences: different staff structures; differing scales of provisions; a collision of cultures (the British Tommy and his immediate superiors regarded the Japanese private soldier as an ignorant 'coolie' while the Japanese thought the British were a lot of unwashed barbarians). But there were also very practical battlefield issues that went unresolved, not least that, in the heat of battle, Japanese soldiers could not always distinguish British soldiers from German ones. Kamio's tactical use of British troops also dismayed Brigadier-General Barnardiston who wrote to his commanders in London:

> I learned that the Japanese commander wished to use the force under my command in the centre of the line, and he desired me, therefore, to march via Chimo and Liutung towards Litsung [*sic*] ... To comply ... implied a very heavy strain on my transport and probably very short rations, as it implied a line of communications nearly 40 miles in length, over a single, bad, narrow and congested road, or rather track. It was essential, however, to make the effort and I decided to do so, even if we had to exist on half-rations.

The Royal Navy, on the other hand, were getting on famously with their Japanese counterparts and HMS *Triumph* played her full part in the bombardment of Tsingtao from the sea. Yet while blanket shelling could cover Japanese forces involved in specific operations, it had not destroyed the coastal batteries, so Kato moved in three of his ships for an attempt at closer range. German return fire drove them away again, however, and on 14

October Kato brought in his entire fleet for a concerted effort. Their main target was Hweichuen Fort but it was a 240mm shell from the battery there that scored the major hit of this particular engagement. It struck the *Triumph* just below the mainmast, killing one sailor and badly wounding two others. The British vessel was temporarily put out of commission. She steamed away to be repaired at sea. She would, though, return to witness the fall of Tsingtao.

From the balcony on the coast commander's post, about half a mile from the fort, Gunther Plüschow witnessed the whole thing. Given the number of Allied shells that whistled over his head towards Hweichuen Fort he feared the worst and when the barrage had eased he was driven up there in the motor car he had been allotted. To his intense relief, the damage to the fort itself had been minimal. True, it was surrounded by shell craters but there had been no loss of life, nor even a man wounded according to his account. He sought out the battery commander, Second Lieutenant Hans Hashagen, and congratulated him on the direct hit on the *Triumph*; the gunners had somehow raised their gun to an even higher angle and gained enough range to score some major damage.

Plüschow also found the fort's commander, Lieutenant Wilhelm Kopp, and they exchanged ideas about what they would do when the war was over. It was decided that Plüschow would march in the victory parade through Berlin side-by-side with the gallant defenders of the Hweichuen Fort with whom he felt a special bond.

The following day, the peninsula was struck by another typhoon. Fifteen inches of rain fell in only two days, washing away the narrow-gauge railway and eroding the new gun plat-forms, all of which set the Allies back by several days. Twenty-five Japanese soldiers were drowned in flash floods.

Earlier in October, a short truce had been arranged so that non-combatants could be evacuated and the dead buried. The evacuees left on the little steamer *Tsimo*. Entertained on the short journey by III Seebattalion's band, they were taken just across the bay to Tuan-tau, off the southernmost tip of the peninsula. Two female nurses were the only Germans who elected to leave. Willys Ruggles Peck, the Tientsin-born American consul who had been in the post for only five months, wanted to stay but was ordered by Washington to depart. The American journalist A M Brace of the Associated Press remained. Plüschow would later meet Brace in the most unusual circumstances. In the meantime, the American was the only journalist in Tsingtao and he was enjoying the grandstand view.

The non-combatants gone, the crews of all non-essential ships in Tsingtao harbour were landed; it was planned that they would be used as infantry when the final assault came. The sailors stood and watched as their ships, which included the *Lauting*, were scuttled. The *Cormoran*, *Iltis* and *Luchs* had already endured similar fates, being tied together and then towed to deep water where they were blown up.

On the night of 17 October, *S-90* slipped out of harbour in attempt to run the blockade. Again, Plüschow was one of the officers who grouped in the coast commander's stand to watch events unfold. At just after 11pm on that clear, moonless night, *S-90* stole out of Tsingtao. Two hours went by and there was no gunfire, no searchlights: *S-90* seemed to have made it. Then suddenly there was a huge explosion and a fireball. She had fired three torpedoes at the Naniwa Class light cruiser *Takachiho*, detonating the magazine. The fire could be seen 20 miles away and the *Takachiho* sank with the loss of 271 officers and men including her captain, Ito Sukeyasu. It would be the largest single loss for Japanese forces during the entire war.

In the mayhem that followed, *S-90*, also damaged in the explosion, sped away into the night. Helmut Brunner decided that there was no chance of returning to Tsingtao, and as she had fired her last torpedo and was leaking, he took *S-90* 60 miles south before beaching her on Chinese soil, an occurrence that caused several diplomatic incidents. First, the local authorities raised the Chinese flag on *S-90*; then the Japanese landed a seaplane and raised their own flag on her. Eventually, the

Japanese took down the flag but left a gunboat to guard over the torpedo boat, claiming that they had also found German mine charts on her, an unlikely event since, even if Brunner had been so careless, the Chinese had got there first and would surely have discovered such a treasure. The *S-90*'s crew, meanwhile, were interned in Nanking, which brought forth a storm of German protests that they should be returned to Germany. A few weeks later, Gunther Plüschow would renew acquaintance with them.

On 25 October, as the weather cleared, Kamio's siege artillery reported itself ready for action. The Japanese commander had planned a seven-day bombardment before the final land assault but first Kato's fleet began to pound Tsingtao's sea batteries. HMS *Triumph*, now repaired, joined in and two days' of intense shelling reduced the batteries to rubble.

On the 28th, the Japanese made another bit of military history when four aircraft – two from the Navy, two from the Army – took advantage of the full moon to carry out the world's first night-time bombing raid, on Iltis Platz and Tsingtao harbour. There was hardly any damage, although Plüschow later complained about the loss of sleep.

Finally, on 31 October, Kamio's land artillery opened fire with a massive bombardment that lasted all day. Sailors landed from the *Kaiserin Elisabeth* were among the casualties, including the Hungarian ordinary seaman József Ács, who was killed after a direct hit on the battery to which he had been assigned. His shipmate, Bélak Domokos, was wounded and would eventually join the rest of the *Kaiserin Elisabeth*'s crew in the prison camp on the island of Ninoshima.

The defenders abandoned their shattered batteries and that night the enemy dug in 300yds nearer to the German last line. The bombardment continued well into the first day of November, this time targeting oil tanks and the docks. The remaining land batteries were destroyed while Kato's fleet finished off the sea batteries. Again at night, the Japanese moved forward and on 2 November Meyer-Waldeck ordered the scuttling of the *Kaiserin Elisabeth* and the *Jaguar*. Only her captain,

71

chief engineer and fifteen sailors had remained on board the *Kaiserin Elisabeth* which now sailed to the deepest point of the bay. She went down in the small hours of 3 November, colours still flying.

During the previous day Japanese artillery, its work on the German heavy batteries done, shifted its sights to the redoubts, one of which had already exchanged fire with a Japanese patrol that was cutting through its barbed wire. Again, the invaders dug forward – they had progressed some 650yds in two nights – and at dawn on 4 November Japanese infantry took the secondary water pumping station at Haipo Creek, leaving the besieged Germans with mostly well water to drink since the main pumping station at Litsun had been badly damaged by artillery fire a month earlier. When electric power was lost and the remaining pumps at Litsun stopped, fighting fires became a real problem.

Still the bombardment continued, flattening barbed wire, smashing the redoubts and, for good measure, reducing the already out-of-action batteries to rubble. Throughout it all, Plüschow flew his Taube, evading ever-increasing enemy fire and then somehow bringing the aircraft safely down before being driven at breakneck speed to Bismarck Fort to report the latest enemy positions.

On the night of 4–5 November, the Japanese dug forward yet another 300yds but the British force, exposed to fire on a slope and unable to dig because of a high water table, lost two Sepoys from the 36th Sikhs killed and eighteen wounded (including men from the South Wales Borderers) before they were forced to withdraw.

On 5 November, the Japanese Second Fleet, now untroubled by German guns, was able to move in close and destroy the last major sea battery, at Hweichuen Fort. With some of the redoubts abandoned and the last of the barbed wire flattened in the mud, Tsingtao now had no effective defences left. That night, the Japanese dug their final assault parallel, in some sectors only 100yds from German trenches, most which were already filled not with men but with rubble. That night the South Wales Borderers had eight killed and twenty-four wounded and the Sikhs again suffered casualties.

Down in Tsingtao, the hospitals and first-aid stations filled up with German wounded. Communications between the defenders was almost impossible because most of the town's telephone wires were down. Sleep was definitely impossible as the barrage continued day and night. Gunther reflected that the Japanese artillery had done a fine job, but then he was not surprised since many of their gunnery officers had been trained by Germans at the Imperial School of Artillery at Jüterbog near Berlin. The Japanese also dropped leaflets, effectively warning the Germans that if they continued to destroy ships, weapons and other equipment, they would pay a high price for denying these to the victors.

On 5 November, Meyer-Waldeck ordered Gunther Plüschow to fly to neutral China. The previous day Plüschow had destroyed the little seaplane that Viktor Klobucar had helped him build from spare parts and serviceable bits of Müllerskowski's damaged Taube, for use when the Iltis Platz airfield became too dangerous to use because of enemy fire. The two-seater biplane had never flown and now Plüschow was going to have to brave Japanese artillery and make one last take-off from the airstrip. Meyer-Waldeck told him that the Japanese attack was expected at any time. He gave Plüschow a bundle of documents to deliver somehow into German hands, and then handed him a passport written in both German and Chinese

Gunther returned to his villa, where he had been living alone since the siege intensified. Patzig's duties meant that he had to remain at his battery, and soon after the first shots were fired, Fritz, Max and August had fled, shortly to be followed by Maurice, the cook. A few days later a new cook, William, had appeared on the scene and the promise of a pay rise had ensured his services until he, too, took to his heels after one shell landed uncomfortably close to the villa. Simon had left with Patzig, but Dorsch remained there for a while, keeping Gunther company as the two moved their beds to the corner of a downstairs room, well away from the windows.

Now Plüschow gathered up what possessions he could reasonably take with him, undid the stable door and let Fips have his freedom, released his chickens from their coop, and then, after one last look around the place that had been his home for far too short a time, made his way down to the hanger to prepare the Taube for its last flight from Tsingtao. Afterwards he pored over his maps, deciding on the best route, and that evening went up to see his friend Julius Aye, a lieutenant twenty months Plüschow's junior who was commanding a small battery that was under almost constant shellfire. Gunther looked out over Tsingtao and was transfixed by the panorama spread out below him. Flashes of fire from the guns were followed a split second later by thunderous roars and then the shells whistled over his head. There was now little return fire coming the other way, but out on the southernmost point of Tsingtao, the battery at Hsiauniwa Fort still blazed away defiantly. Then it was time to go. Gunther shook Aye's hand and wished him well. Two days later Aye was dead.

In the early dawn of 6 November 1914, Gunther Plüschow shook hands with each of the four men who had helped him prepare the Taube, then stroked the head of his dog, Husdent, for the last time. He climbed into the tiny cockpit, started the engine, and then opened the throttle of the aircraft, which bounced down what passed for a runway. He gave his signal for the final time, the ground crew released the rope and Plüschow was slung-shot into the air. The machine had reached about 250ft when it was thrown violently by a shell blast. Plüschow saw a large hole had appeared in his port wing where a splinter had torn straight through the fabric. More enemy fire followed him as he climbed up and away, then he was high enough to level out. He looked back at Tsingtao and could see clearly the battle below him, flashes of fire marking the opposing lines like a model on a table in some military schoolroom. Black smoke billowed from the burning oil tanks. But the sun was rising and he turned towards Cape Taschke.

As Plüschow flew south, Japanese guns at land and on sea continued to pound Tsingtao. The invaders were running out of targets but they kept up the barrage anyway as German morale crumbled with the last of the masonry. The final assault would surely come at any time, but the ever-cautious Kamio wanted the British to close up his line and join the attack. He ordered Barnardiston to dig the final saps and parallels at all costs. Japanese infantry would provide covering fire.

Barnardiston reported back to London:

> I considered it my duty to represent to the Japanese Commander-in-Chief the untenable nature, for permanent occupation, of the third position in my front, but received a reply that it was necessary for it to be held in order for it to fit in with the general scheme of the assault. On the evening of the 6th, I accordingly occupied it with piquets, and the working parties continued to improve it.

Major Ernest Knox of the 36th Sikhs later complained about Japanese non-commissioned soldiers' 'appalling carelessness in dealing with explosives'.

Local firefights around the remaining redoubts now became the main feature of the advance until a gap appeared in the centre of the line, through which Japanese forces fanned out.

Barnardiston described the final few hours:

> During the night, on hearing rumours of the evacuation of one or more of the redoubts, I sent out officers' patrols to ascertain if the enemy were still holding the trenches in

front of us, and prepared to advance should the front be clear. They were met, however, with rifle and machine gun fire, and reported that No. 2 Redoubt, on our left, was still held.

Between 5am and 6am on the morning of the 7th, the enemy started a further cannonade for field artillery and an occasional shot from their heavy guns, and I issued preparatory orders for an advance as soon as I knew that the redoubts were captured. At 7am all firing ceased, and I was informed that the enemy had sent out a flag of truce.

About 7.30am I received orders to advance, and, the enemy along the whole of our front line having then retired, I marched into Tsingtao.

In fact, Meyer-Waldeck had surrendered Tsingtao at 6.23am. There was absolutely no point in going on. White flags were run up on Signal Hill and at various other points. Then three figures came out. Major Georg von Kayser, the interpreter, was on horseback, led by a foot soldier. A bugler, also on foot, carried a white flag. Von Kayser had with him a communiqué from Meyer-Waldeck addressed to the Japanese Commander-in-Chief. Tsingtao's defences now exhausted, the Governor was ready to enter into surrender negotiations. If Kamio agreed to this, then Meyer-Waldeck would nominate Ludwig Saxer, the Tsingtao Chief of Staff, as his chief negotiator.

It was a perilous mission because heavy firing was still going on. A stray bullet killed the bugler, and von Kayser's horses were shot from under him. Eventually, the major delivered the document, and that afternoon the two sides met formally at Moltke Barracks (Bismarck Fort was badly damaged and burning) where surrender terms were agreed. However, in the confusion and noise of a still fierce battle, putting an end to the fighting was not an easy task. Several German posts refused to give in immediately and the last casualties were two British soldiers, killed by a German shell. That was ironic as well as tragic because it was the British who were given the honour of marching into the city.

This was not a grand gesture on Kamio's part. He just did not have time to reorganize his troops into a parade. The British were better placed.

Three days later, a Japanese torpedo boat sank while sweeping mines. The defenders of Tsingtao suffered 199 dead, including 10 from the Austro-Hungarian *Kaiserin Elisabeth*, and 294 wounded; altogether about 3,800 were taken prisoner. According to the most reliable accounts, the Japanese land forces suffered 1,900 casualties (415 dead) and lost the *Takachiho*, and the *Shirotaye*, as well as a torpedo boat and two small minesweepers with some 300 dead and 100 wounded. British casualties (13 Army and 3 Navy dead, plus 74 Army and 9 Navy wounded) were disproportionately high to the number of troops involved. Mitsuomi Kamio's cautionary tactics had certainly been justified as Japan paid a remarkably low price for seizing such a prize.

The Japanese now began to clear the debris, make safe unexploded shells and bombs (it would take weeks), and change all road signs and street names into Japanese. German prisoners were taken to Japan to be interned for the duration (Meyer-Waldeck was put aboard the coal ship *Satsuma Maru* for the first part of his journey to the POW camp at Fukuoka on the northern shore of the island of Kyushu) while Willys Peck returned to reopen the American consulate (it was shut down again in April 1916) and Reginald Eckford also returned, to find a Japanese flag flying over what had been the British consulate; he simply relocated.

Gunther Plüschow, meanwhile, was having his own adventures in China.

Chapter 9

Crash Landing

After he left the burning protectorate Gunther Plüschow had planned to fly first to the town of Haichow, 155 miles to the south-west of Tsingtao, just over the border in Kiangsu province on a small river 18 miles inland from the Yellow Sea. There he hoped to refuel before continuing to Shanghai where he had German friends. Guided by map and compass, he arrived over Haichow at about 8am but the typhoon rains of late summer that had continued into late autumn had left many square miles of the flat, low-lying area around the town flooded. Plüschow flew on for several miles before turning back to his original destination and, once there, circling around for several minutes, trying to find a suitable landing place. The dry areas all appeared to be covered either by dwellings or burial mounds but eventually he spotted a small field that had apparently been drained. It was going to be a tight squeeze, not least because the field was bounded either by walls, ditches or the Haichow River, but he had no choice, not least because his fuel gauge was touching almost empty

Drawing on his experiences in landing at Iltis Platz, Plüschow brought the Taube down in wide circles until, at 8.45am, it touched the ground – and promptly sank into thick, sticky mud. Its wheels stuck fast, the aircraft came to a shuddering halt and tipped up on to its nose, its propeller, already repaired many times, shattering upon impact. The pilot, though, could be pleased that he was still in one piece and that for once his descent had not been to the accompaniment of artillery shells.

For a few moments, silence reigned in the morning sun, then a cock crowed and suddenly he was aware of people running towards him. It was not unlike the scene at the little village in Germany where he had made his unscheduled appearance earlier that year. In moments he was surrounded by a crowd of excited locals, none of who had ever seen an aircraft before and all of who kept a safe distance from this machine and its strange occupant that had landed on the edge of their town. It crossed Plüschow's mind that these were simple people who might think he was an evil spirit, so he tried a friendly gesture. That did not work, so he dug into his pocket and threw some coins towards them. This seemed to calm matters and Plüschow was wondering what his next move should be, when he heard someone calling out in English. Through the crowd of chattering Chinese men, women and children strode a man who introduced himself as Dr Lorenzo S Morgan, an American medical missionary who, with his wife, Dr Ruth Bennett Morgan, was working in China on behalf of the Presbyterian Church in the USA. The American spoke the local dialect and enlisted some onlookers to help tip the Taube back into a horizontal position.

Without fuel or propeller, the aircraft was going nowhere but Plüschow still removed the steering wheel and then, with his Mauser pistol and package of papers, he climbed down from the Taube. He handed to Morgan the passport that Alfred von Meyer-Waldeck had provided for him and the American sent the document straight off to the local mandarin. It was as well, he told Plüschow, to make a friend of this official, effectively the local magistrate who enjoyed far-reaching powers. Soon, a squad of about forty soldiers arrived to guard the Taube, and Plüschow felt able to leave for the Morgans' home.

The Americans made him welcome and over breakfast he learned that they had both graduated as physicians from the John Hopkins Medical School. They had married in Nashville, Tennessee, in June 1904 and, apart from a visit back to the USA in 1911–12 to continue studying medicine, they had spent almost their entire married life in China. An infant son had died in 1907 but they now had two daughters, the youngest of which had been born at the hospital in Tsingtao just four months before

Plüschow's unscheduled visit to their home. In fact, Ruth Morgan had been in the colony giving birth at the very time the Taube was being assembled. An avid photographer, she was now keen to take some pictures of the aircraft.

That, though, would have to wait. A Chinese officer had arrived at the Morgans' home to announce that a guard of honour had been placed outside their house. The mandarin would call upon their guest in half an hour. Before then, however, there were other visitors, other civilian officials from the town. With Lorenzo Bennett acting as interpreter, Plüschow answered their questions. Where had he come from? Was it true that he had flown through the air? How long had it taken? And how were things in Tsingtao? The German wished that he knew the answer to that one.

When the mandarin arrived, he did so with great ceremony and to the accompaniment of drums and whistles. He enquired of Plüschow's health, asked him what were his wishes, and assured the German that everything would be done to help and protect the visitor. Before he left, again with great ceremony, the mandarin invited the flying man to dine with him that evening. Plüschow accepted, then went back to his aircraft and began to dismantle it, watched by Ruth Morgan who took photographs of the proceedings.

Taking the Taube apart proved an even bigger job than had assembling it, not least because tools were in short supply. All Plüschow had to work with was an axe and an ancient saw, both of which he borrowed from the American mission. Now dressed in his civilian clothes, he had already planned to present his Mauser to the mandarin and, after four hours of toil to remove the Mercedes engine from the Taube, he decided to hand over that as well. He wanted to take the rest of the aircraft intact into the walled town but first the wings had to be removed. Even then, what was left would not fit through the gates, so Plüschow resigned himself to the inevitable: he doused the aircraft in petrol and set it alight.

Then, the sad task done, he prepared for his evening appointment with the mandarin, an event that turned out to be far grander than he could possibly have imagined. The mandarin's personal litter was sent to collect him and eight muscular men carried him on the forty-minute journey with soldiers, bayonets fixed, marching alongside. Torches, lanterns and – to German ears at least – discordant Chinese music all added to the pomp, the only interruption to which came when the bearers moved the carrying poles to their other shoulders; and even that was done with some ceremony when the man at the head of the procession signalled the change-over by rapping his stick on the ground. At the mandarin's residence, the music and lights continued, local military and civilian dignitaries lined up to welcome him, and a sumptuous banquet was served, the guest of honour losing count after the arrival of the thirty-sixth course. Then, with Lorenzo Morgan again acting as interpreter, Plüschow answered everyone's questions about the battle for Tsingtao and his own exploits as an aviator.

The evening ended, Plüschow was told that, as a matter of pure formality, he would be taken to Nanking before his onward journey to Shanghai from where could join a ship. The following day he bid farewell to his hosts and was escorted to one of two junks that lay on the Haichow River. His quarters were bare, the weather had dropped cold and he would have been in considerable discomfort had it not been for the warm clothing, sleeping bag and blankets given to him by the Morgans. It was yet another generous gesture by the American couple and quite how he would have fared without their help he dared not contemplate.

Chapter 10

Mr McGarvin

In mid-November 1914, Gunther Plüschow arrived in Nanking, the city that three years earlier had become the capital of the new Republic of China. Nanking stood on the south bank of the Yangtze River, 189 miles north-west of Shanghai, and the journey from Haichow had taken well over five days. From the Haichow River to the Grand Canal coolies had pulled the little convoy of junks. Then the wind picked up and the square matting sails could be raised for the journey up the great Yangtze, the third-longest river in the world. Apart from the junks' crews, Plüschow's companions had numbered forty-five rank-and-file soldiers, two junior officers and their commanding officer General Liu who, the German learned, boasted a fearsome reputation as the scourge of the river pirates who infested the Yangtze. Occasionally, the general had joined Plüschow as he walked along the bank, and they had shared meals, both activities carried out in polite silence as neither could speak a word of the other's language.

Eventually, Plüschow had managed to get hold of a copy of the English-language newspaper, the *Shanghai Times*, in which he was appalled to read accounts of the fall of Tsingtao which reported a cowardly capitulation by a drunken and ill-disciplined German garrison. In fact the paper had always followed a pro-Japanese policy and was supported by Japanese money, even though the owner was British. Plüschow said later that he had thrown the newspaper away in disgust, but one truth he had learned was that the colony had fallen soon after his own flight from it.

There was one moment, however, that brightened his arrival in

Nanking: the welcome he received from Helmut Brunner, the commander of the torpedo boat *S-90*. After scuttling the boat, Brunner and his crew, guarded by Chinese troops, had trekked over the mountains before being put on a train for Nanking. Now Brunner accompanied Plüschow to the building where he and his men were being held. To Plüschow's surprise a room had already been prepared for the latest arrival, and then he realized what was happening: like the crew of *S-90*, he was to be interned.

Plüschow protested. That was not what he had been told. He was to go to Shanghai; the stop at Nanking was just a formality. He found General Liu again and insisted on being taken to the governor's residence. The general accompanied him there but the governor was not available. Instead, an elderly official wished Plüschow the very best of good fortune and expressed the hope that the German would be comfortable in the city. Plüschow turned to Liu but the general, his mission completed, made no attempt to hide the fact that he was anxious to begin his journey back to Haichow. As he climbed back into the carriage for his own journey to rejoin Brunner, Plüschow was taken aback when an armed Chinese soldier stepped up behind him. When he again protested, Plüschow was told that the soldier was his guard of honour and, henceforth, would accompany him at all times. Internment or just plain house arrest, Plüschow knew that his war was likely to end here unless he took matters into his own hands – with a little help from his friends, of course.

That evening, along with the officers from *S-90*, he was invited to the home of a German resident of Nanking. Again his shadow was just a pace or two behind him. At around 10pm, his colleagues bid their goodnights and returned to their quarters, their own guards close behind. After about thirty minutes the houseboy was sent out to tell Plüschow's guardian that everyone had left. What was he still doing here? At this point it may have occurred to the sentry that all Westerners looked the same to a Chinese foot soldier. Whatever, he did not wait to check. Instead he shot off in a panic, trying to catch up with the German officer he had been deputed to watch. As soon as the

The proud young naval officer: Gunther Plüschow in 1906. (*Plüschow*)

MS *Fürst Bismarck*, the flagship on which Gunther Plüschow first served on the China tion. (*Author's Collection*)

A little bit of Germany by the sea: Tsingtao pictured on the eve of the First World War. (*Bundesarchiv*)

German officers horse racing at Tsingtao. Gunther Plüschow had to use the racecourse as a makeshift airfield. (*Bundesarchiv*)

Japanese forces land at Laoshan Bay to the north Tsingtao in September 19 (*Author's Collection*)

Plüschow's Rumpler Taube outside the walls of Haichow. (*Dr Ruth Bennett Morgan*)

Plüschow presents the engine of the Taube to th local mandarin at Haich (*Dr Ruth Bennett Morgan*)

sad moment: Plüschow with his burning Taube. (*Dr Ruth Bennett Morgan*)

ischow poses in the clothes he wore during
escape from London. (*Plüschow*)

Mr McGarvin on board the *Mongolia* as it
reaches the United States. (*Plüschow*)

The liner *Andania* was used as a prison ship in the Solent. It was Gunther Plüschow's first 'home' when he arrived in England. (*Author's Collection*)

A newspaper artist's impressions of life at Dorchester POW camp in 1915. (*Author's Collection*)

German prisoners attract much attention as they are marched through the streets of Castle Donington on their way to Donington Hall in 1915. (*Author's Collection*)

nington Hall camp,
tately home
rounded by a wire
ce. (*Author's Collection*)

German officers enjoy
a game of football in
the shadow of their
Donington prison.
(*Author's Collection*)

Two German officers
engrossed in a game
of chess at Donington
Hall. (*W W Winter*)

Gunther Plüschow and Isot are married in an aircraft hanger at Libau in June 1916. (*Plüschow*)

A portrait of Gunther Plüschow taken in 1930 before he returned to South America for the l time. (*Archiv Gerhard H Ehlers, Odenthal*)

Gunther Plüschow (third from the right) hosts a visit by the Kaiserin, Princess Auguste Viktoria, the air base at Kiel-Holtenau in 1916. (*Plüschow*)

(*Top*) The Heinkel HD 24W – the *Silberkondor* – pictured in the bay at Ushuaia. (*Archiv Gerhard H Ehlers, Odenthal*)

(*Left*) The *Feuerland* that took Plüschow and his party halfway around the world. (*Archiv Gerhard H Ehlers, Odenthal*)

The *Silberkondor* in the harbour at Punta Arenas, December 1928. Gunther Plüschow is standing on the left. (*Archiv Gerhard H Ehlers, Odenthal*)

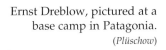

Ernst Dreblow, pictured at a base camp in Patagonia. (*Plüschow*)

The *Silberkondor* dwarfed
by its surroundings.
(*Plüschow*)

The legend lives on: advertisement for
the film *Ikarus* that was released after
Plüschow's death. (*Author's Collection*)

Newspaper cutting reporting the interment of Gunther
Plüschow's ashes at the Park Cemetery in the Berlin
suburb of Lichterfelde. (*Landesarchiv Berlin*)

Totenfeier für Gunther Plüschow.

In einer erhebenden Feier gestaltete sich auf dem Lichterfelder Parkfriedhof die Beisetzung Gunther
Plüschows und seines mit ihm über Feuerland abgestürzten Flugkameraden Dreblow. Unser
zeigt die feierliche Ueberführung der Urnen zur Grabstätte.

guard was out of sight, a carriage was brought round and Plüschow was driven to the railway station. There he bought a ticket for the express to Shanghai. He knew that in the international community that had overwhelmed the city there might well be British people that he had met in Tsingtao before the war. But Shanghai was his only real hope of escape.

Through a combination of Chinese and British finance, the Shanghai–Nanking Railway had been completed in 1908 and was probably the country's most vital rail service, connecting the most important financial centre in the Far East (already home to more than one million people) to the capital of the new republic. Transporting foreign businessmen from one to the other was its core business and it would have been no surprise to Plüschow that, when he knocked on the door of the last available sleeping compartment, an Englishman opened it. The man, who had been roused from his slumber, was in no mood for conversation so Plüschow gratefully climbed up into the remaining berth and turned off the light. He could not sleep, though. Every time the train stopped at a station, he half-expected the door to burst open and to be hauled down from his bunk.

Dawn was breaking when the train pulled into the Shanghai–Nanking Railway Company's station at the end of its journey. The ticket collector did not seem particularly interested in him, so Plüschow walked on through the station's mix of Chinese and Western architecture and out into the wide street where he summoned a rickshaw and was soon speeding along through the Chinese quarter, again not feeling at all relaxed until he reached the European area. He went straight to the home of a German acquaintance, where, for the first time in days, weeks probably, he felt safe.

Over the next three weeks, Plüschow was introduced to several of his fellow countrymen, including one man with whom he had something in common. Otto Wiesinger, a 30-year-old military reservist who, before the war, had been an importer with business interests in Shanghai, had also escaped from Tsingtao. When the Japanese arrived, Wiesinger had been in hospital there, recovering from dysentery. He had been reasonably well treated by the invaders and eventually managed to flee disguised as a Chinese.

Plüschow moved to a succession of 'safe houses', always adopting a different identity until the daughter of a diplomat he knew from Berlin obtained for him a passport in the name of a Mr E F McGarvin, a representative of the Singer Sewing Machine Company, the sales and distribution division of Singer Manufacturing, together with money and a ticket on a ship leaving for the United States.

Now he needed to lay a false trail, even among the German community, and so began to express fears for his safety in Shanghai. When he finally said his goodbyes, he told his compatriots that he would be travelling by train to Peking, where he would present himself at the German embassy. There might even be a position for him there, he told them.

In fact, Plüschow's closest friends had arranged for him to be driven to the Wusong River and then taken by boat to a factory area downstream, where he was shown to a small room in an apartment block. According to his later account, a member of one of the 'Entente' nations also lived in building and Plüschow feigned madness in order to keep him from prying into the affairs of his new neighbour. Now there was a waiting game to play. Plüschow, or rather McGarvin, had been booked to sail on the SS *Mongolia*, a 13,638-ton passenger-and-cargo liner of the Pacific Mail Steamship Company which was due to leave for San Francisco on 5 December 1914. Plüschow whiled away the next three days by playing the madman, occasionally stamping about his tiny room, at other times slumping in his chair staring straight ahead when his food was delivered. He began to enjoy the foolishness of it all. He had nothing else to occupy his mind and it amused him, especially when the boy who brought his meals pushed the tray into the room and then beat a hasty retreat, scrabbling to lock the door behind him.

Eventually it was time to board, but Mr McGarvin had to overcome the fact that he was undertaking such a long journey with only one piece of luggage, especially as he had been booked into a state cabin. It was something that would alert a vigilant crew member, so Plüschow decided that the best form of defence was attack. He demanded to know of the cabin steward whether all his other belongings had been carefully handled when they were brought aboard the previous day. Of course they had, he was assured.

The *Mongolia* slipped out of Shanghai harbour in good weather, despite the bad sea of the previous day, and Mr McGarvin – a gregarious sort of chap surely, if he were a salesman – might have been expected to spend the voyage mixing with his fellow passengers. But there were still several hurdles for Plüschow to negotiate before the *Mongolia* set off across the Pacific, not least the three Japanese ports where she was scheduled to call, the first of which was Nagasaki, a major base for the Imperial Japanese Navy.

A few hours into the voyage, as the Mongolia steamed across the East China Sea towards Japan, Mr McGarvin was taken ill and the ship's American doctor summoned. Plüschow was taking a chance but when he explained his true situation, the doctor agreed to help. The stewards were told that Mr McGarvin was a sick man. He would be unable to leave his bed for several days. All meals would have to be brought to his cabin. If he wanted anything else, then the duty steward should send for the doctor. Thus, three days later when the ship docked at Nagasaki to take on coal, and Japanese officials boarded her and assembled the passengers in the saloon to question them and check their documents, one passenger was missing. When the absentee's name was called, it was the *Mongolia*'s doctor who stepped forward to explain: Mr McGarvin had a high fever and the doctor believed that he was suffering from a highly contagious disease. The explanation did not satisfy the port officials and the ship's doctor was asked to produce the patient to a Japanese doctor.

Accompanied by two policemen, the doctors went to Mr McGarvin's cabin where the invalid lay huddled under his bedclothes, moaning and groaning. It was enough to convince the Japanese policemen who beat a hasty retreat, and even the doctor did not appear keen to make his own examination.

That afternoon, Plüschow got up and looked out of his port-hole. He had visited Nagasaki before the war; now he wanted another glimpse. Situated on the island of Kyushu, the city lay at the head of a long bay that formed a wonderful natural harbour. When Plüschow had last been here, he would have seen workmen building the Ukrami Cathedral. The cathedral had been completed earlier in 1914, the largest Catholic church in all of East Asia. But, he wrote later, it was not the city's skyline that grabbed his attention now; it was the activity in the harbour and on the quayside. Soldiers, horses and weaponry were being put ashore, and the dockside was lined with flags. That evening he managed to obtain a copy of an English-language newspaper that trumpeted Japan's victory over Germany. Of course, it was not only Tsingtao and Kiaochow Bay that had fallen under Japan's control; it also held the German Micronesian Islands over a huge swathe of the Pacific. The Japanese had every reason to celebrate. Gunther Plüschow had every reason to feel angry as he watched them do so.

Altogether the *Mongolia* spent five days in Japanese waters, calling also at Kobe and Yokohama. At each port the same charade was enacted: officials came on board, asked to see the absent passenger, and were escorted the cabin where he writhed in agony in his bed. And each time they left just as hastily as had their counterparts in Nagasaki.

Once the *Mongolia* was in neutral waters, Mr McGarvin achieved a remarkable recovery. He was up and about, taking the air on deck, and enjoying the company of his fellow passengers who numbered among them several German civilians whose business had taken them to China, as well as a brother German officer who had been seconded to Shanghai. Quite why the Japanese had not bothered with them is unclear, although it had been reported that German officers held prisoner in Nagasaki after the fall of various German possessions had in fact been free to walk round the city at will, provided that they were safely back in their hotels and houses by dusk. But Plüschow, of course, the Dragon Pilot of Tsingtao, would have been a prize catch. His decision to hide had been a wise one.

As the *Mongolia* steamed on towards Honolulu, the Dragon Pilot renewed acquaintance with someone else who had survived the siege of Tsingtao. The Associated Press correspondent, A M Brace, had left the colony shortly after the Japanese took over. The journalist probably could not believe his good fortune. Here he was, the only newspaperman aboard a ship on which the well-known German pilot was also travelling, and with days to interview his subject. Brace made the most of the opportunity and on 23 December 1914, the day after the Mongolia had docked in Honolulu, the *Pacific Commercial Advertiser*, the island's biggest newspaper, took time off from reporting on plans to reclaim Waikiki's duck ponds, to tell its readers: 'Eye Witness Relates How Teutons Lost At Tsingtau.'

Brace's own account of the siege and its aftermath was gripping stuff in which Plüschow's escapades received plenty of coverage. Yet the correspondent stated that he was unable to confirm reports that the daring aviator who 'did heroic work for the Fatherland' was indeed travelling on the *Mongolia* under the name of E F McGarvin. The reason for the subterfuge is quite unclear. Perhaps it was at Plüschow's insistence that, in return for helping Brace with his article, his own identity remained a secret, for the moment at least.

Perhaps not: Plüschow wrote later that, after the ship had left on the final leg of its journey to San Francisco, he had to take Brace to task after the reporter showed him a copy of the local newspaper that, in great detail, 'recounted all my misdeeds during and after the siege of Tsingtao'.

In the meantime, in Honolulu, Plüschow was initially delighted to see a small German cruiser in the harbour, although she was not flying the usual military flags. The *Geier* had an interesting story. Upon the outbreak of war, the cruiser had been ordered to join von Spee's East Asia Squadron out of Tsingtao. But the squadron had already departed and the *Geier*'s captain decided that his unprotected ship's best course of action would be to find a neutral port. Somehow the cruiser evaded capture and sailed the thousands of miles to Pearl Harbor.

On 8 November 1914, the *New York Times* reported:

> The little German cruiser *Geier*, which has been repairing at Honolulu, while a Japanese [ship] waited outside the harbour for her to reappear on the high seas, was interned for the war at Honolulu last midnight, the time set by the American government for her to interne or leave port . . . the case of the *Geier* aroused much international interest. Soon after she dropped anchor in the harbour at Honolulu, about three weeks ago, after a voyage from the Far East, a powerful Japanese cruiser, the *Hisen*, appeared off the Hawaiian coast and anchored outside the three-mile limit. Afterwards, another Japanese cruiser joined the *Hisen* and they seemed determined to wait as long as necessary for the enemy. These cruisers can now join in the general search for German warships in the Pacific.

In fact, the *Geier* spent the next three years interned in Honolulu until the United States entered the war in 1917. When it became evident that the German crew intended to scuttle their ship, she was seized by an armed party from the USS *St Louis*. It appeared that the Germans had not been idle during their stay: they had been relaying messages between Berlin and Mexico and Canada, in which Germany was attempting to provoke the two nations into hostile action against the United States. The crew were taken as prisoners of war to Fort Douglas in Utah and the *Geier* became the property of the US Navy, undergoing armament modifications before re-entering service as the USS *Schurz*. On 21 June 1918, the *Schurz* sank with the loss of one life after colliding with the SS *Florida*, off the North Carolina coast.

Plüschow was delighted to be able to meet some of the *Geier*'s crew, and even renew some old friendships, but eventually he had to bid them farewell. Then, when Brace showed him that newspaper, he began to worry. When they reached San Francisco, the Americans might arrest him on the strength of Brace's words, although quite why they should, he wasn't sure. The USA had remained neutral in the conflict, he told himself again and again. It was a view supported by several American passengers who assured Plüschow that everyone would regard his adventure in Tsingtao as just that: a rollicking good adventure story. In fact, if he cared to, he could quite likely remain in the United States and make a decent living from writing about his experiences. A sort of lecture tour might even be possible, where he could travel from city to city, recounting his time during the siege and his subsequent escape.

On Tuesday, 29 December 1914, the SS *Mongolia* docked in San Francisco. The ship's passenger manifest now listed the disembarking Mr McGarvin – still with his one piece of checked luggage – by his real name, so the need for subterfuge appears to have ended. On the quayside, dozens of reporters and photographers milled about waiting for their first glimpse of Lieutenant Gunther Plüschow of the Imperial German Navy, the daring aviator of Tsingtao. Damn Brace!

Plüschow tried to deal with them politely but the pushing and jostling annoyed him and his only hope of escape was to be curt, not courteous. He barked at the newsmen that he had nothing to say to say to any of them. It appears that Gunther was saving the best part of his story for his own use. In March 1915 an article entitled 'Flying Under Fire' appeared under his own by-line in *Sunset Magazine*, a San Francisco-based publication that had recently been sold by the Southern Pacific Railroad to its employees and which was being changed from a promotional magazine into one that published original articles. Plüschow would presumably have been regarded as an ideal guest writer because, as it transpired, American officials had no interest in him whatsoever. He could go wherever he pleased.

Chapter 11

American Journey

As 1914 drew to a close, the United States of America was still neutral. Two weeks after war had been declared between Britain and Germany, the American president, Woodrow Wilson, addressed Congress and made public US policy: despite the fact that the people of the United States were drawn from many nations, especially the nations now at war, the US must be neutral in fact as well as in name. Wilson told Congress: 'We must be impartial in thought, as well as action, must put a curb upon our sentiments, as well as upon every transaction that might be construed as a preference of one party to the struggle before another.'

America certainly had its own distractions, not least the ongoing revolution in Mexico that, in April, had seen American marines and sailors occupy the port of Veracruz in the Gulf of Mexico. And in late June, when newspapers covered the assassination of Archduke Franz Ferdinand in Sarajevo, the headlines that caused greater interest were those reporting Suffragettes marching on the Capitol in Washington to demand voting rights for women. On a lighter note, at the beginning of December a 26-year-old Jewish American composer and lyricist who went by the name of Irving Berlin opened his first musical, *Watch Your Step*, on Broadway. It gave the world songs like 'Play a Simple Melody' and it was music and entertainment that gave Gunther Plüschow his first taste of life in the United States.

Two days after Plüschow arrived was New Year's Eve and he was invited to spend the occasion at one of San Francisco's swankiest nightclubs. It was an irony that, while he had expected to be arrested the moment he landed, here he was experiencing one of the most enjoyable evenings of his life with music, dancing and beautiful women. Even the officials at the German consulate were surprised at the freedom that this celebrated combatant from a warring nation was being allowed.

And that was the point: Plüschow was still a member of the Imperial German Navy and his country was still at war. He needed to get home. On 2 January 1915, he climbed aboard a train and left San Francisco behind him. His fellow passengers included another German officer – probably the one who had also arrived on the *Mongolia* – and several German civilians who had travelled on the ship. It was a journey that opened up many of the natural wonders of the continent, not least the Grand Canyon where Plüschow gazed in awe at Nature's might, but its purpose was to lead him back to Germany. The train steamed on through deep canyons and alongside the Colorado River in the heart of the Rockies before descending to Denver, then through the farmlands of Iowa before arriving in Chicago. There, Plüschow left the train and caught another that would take him south-east, to Virginia where he had arranged to meet an old friend.

The advice he received there was to travel to New York where there would be the best possible chance of getting aboard a ship bound for Europe. So Plüschow was soon on his way again, this time his train taking him north-east. In New York, he contacted the people who might help him and was disappointed to learn that it would be some weeks before arrangements could be in place for his departure. Thus, he had time to absorb fully the culture of this strange, brash country.

He also had ample opportunity to see how the war was being reported – and it was from a strong anti-German stance. Despite Woodrow Wilson's assertion that the United States government would not, either by word or deed, take sides, America's newspapers displayed no such inhibitions. One agency report, quoting the British Press Bureau in London, was headlined 'Germans Said To Have Shot Many Priests', and went on to describe how Catholic clergy were 'beaten, tortured, hung and executed'. The article was fairly typical of how Germany was being portrayed in the American Press.

Plüschow was naturally upset. He wrote later: 'Hardly a picture, hardly a newspaper . . . did not incite hatred against Germany . . . ' His only consolation, he said, was that his friends and their acquaintances still treated him well, although there was often an element of 'well, while we know that most Germans are barbarians, of course we also know that you aren't like that'.

There was one moment, however, that captured his heart and reminded him of home. He bought a ticket for the Metropolitan Opera House and listened to one act of Engelbert Humperdinck's opera *Hansel and Gretel*. 'German music, German words, German songs', he recalled. But after he stepped out into the street and walked a few yards a cine-projector that was throwing a war newsreel film against a large blank wall confronted him. Again, it was overwhelmingly anti-German, whipping up a storm of hatred among the large crowd of passers-by that had stopped to watch.

Plüschow's desire to get back to Germany had now reached almost fever pitch itself. And it had its frustrations. Given the opportunity to sign on as an ordinary seaman on a Norwegian vessel, he had to turn it down after learning that several of his shipmates would be British.

After three weeks in New York, he was becoming increasingly desperate. But then he was introduced to a character whose precise profession remained unclear but whose talents lay in the art of forging documents. Soon, Gunther Plüschow, who had set off for America as a sewing machine salesman called Mr McGarvin, was preparing to leave the country as a Swiss lock-smith called Ernst Suse. The passport was perfect and on 30 January 1915 Ernst Suse boarded the *Duca degli Abruzzi*, a 7,793-ton vessel of the Navigazione Generale Italiana Line that had arrived in New York five days earlier. The ship had accommodation for 80 first-class passengers, 16 second-class and 1,740 third-class travellers. It was into that mass of steerage that Suse disappeared.

Launched in May 1907, the *Duca degli Abruzzi* had recently resumed on the Genoa–Naples–New York route after service as an Italian auxiliary cruiser and then working the Genoa–River Plate route. According to Plüschow, conditions among the third-class passengers were atrocious. His bunk in a four-man cabin was close to the engines, the portholes were kept shut and the atmosphere was fetid – a Frenchman in the bunk above kept being sick, and a perpetually drunken Englishman smoked his pipe all day. And then there were the bugs. Not in ones and twos but in their scores, hundreds, probably thousands. Plüschow fought a losing battle with them.

The ship was overladen and the sea was rough. Even for a seasoned sailor it was going to be an unpleasant journey and as the ship pitched and rolled its way across the Atlantic, Plüschow could only gaze enviously at the first-class deck. Then he saw a familiar face. The German officer who had left Shanghai with him aboard the *Mongolia* was deep in conversation with two women.

Although they had been in regular contact in New York, each had been sworn to secrecy by their respective helpers. Until they caught each other's gaze on the *Duca degli Abruzzi* neither had been aware that the other was also aboard. Although his brother officer was in first-class, Plüschow eventually managed to speak to him briefly and learned that he was travelling under the guise of a wealthy Dutchman and, like Plüschow, was destined for Naples.

Given the conditions of his berth, Plüschow was not surprised when he went down with a fever. The ship's Italian doctor was summoned, thought that Mr Suse might have malaria, and prescribed a large dose of quinine. Plüschow, whose temperature had soared to 103F, could do nothing but lie in his bunk, try to fight off the fever and regain his strength for whatever lay ahead when the ship reached is final destination. Eventually, he began to feel better and by the time the *Duca degli Abruzzi* reached Gibraltar on 8 February he was able to go on deck. Plüschow never recorded whether he saw the irony of being genuinely ill and unable to leave his cabin when he had, on the earlier voyage from Shanghai to San Francisco, feigned exactly the same symptoms to avoid being detected. As events turned out, it might have served his purpose better if he had also remained in his sickbed when the ship docked in Gibraltar. Here there was no friendly American doctor to vouch for him.

The First World War saw Gibraltar playing a crucial role in the control of the Straits as an assembly point for convoys and as a support base for the supplies to British troops. It was a highly sensitive area and as soon as the *Duca degli Abruzzi* lay to, two ship's boats came out to her and disgorged a party of British sailors led by an officer. They were accompanied by a number of Gibraltar policemen, and an inspection of all non-British and non-Italian passengers began. The first-class travellers were dealt with speedily and politely and eventually it was the turn of the miserable heap of humanity that had been holed up in steerage for most of the voyage across rough seas. Those claiming Swiss nationality were seen in turn and Plüschow felt reasonably confident. After all, he possessed a 'genuine' passport complete with up-to-date photograph. For a few moments it seemed that he had got away with it. The British officer began to question a tall Swiss and the exchange became heated to the point where the officer ordered the man to be detained. But then he waved the others back to their cabins.

However, they had only just turned to leave when a man in civilian clothes appeared on the scene. They learned later that he was an employee of the Thomas Cook travel agency but that he also acted as an interpreter and, Plüschow thought, 'a spy'. He appeared agitated, and insisted that Plüschow and his fellow holders of Swiss passports all be properly searched. The naval officer, he said, could not simply let them go without further investigation. So they were told to remain for closer inspection. When the man saw that Plüschow had no labels on his clothing, he was convinced: 'He is a German spy', he told the officer.

A Swiss first-class passenger was summoned and asked if the remaining 'Swiss' travellers had the right sort of accent.

Plüschow, for one, failed the test miserably, despite concocting an on-the-spot story that his family had left Switzerland when he was an infant. He could speak good Italian, he said, if that was any help. And he proved it. But it was in vain. The officer had been convinced that something was not right. Plüschow was allowed to gather his belongings. Then he was escorted into one of the small naval craft and taken ashore. As the little boat pulled away, he looked up at the ship's rail and saw a familiar face. Looking back at him, a wealthy 'Dutch' gentleman gave Plüschow a faint smile of resignation.

Chapter 12

England

As the little launch butted its way back to Gibraltar's harbour, Gunther Plüschow weighed up his situation. He had left Tsingtao as the Japanese closed in; he had survived a crash landing in China; he had managed to escape from what amounted to house arrest in Nanking; and he had made his way right across the United States and then managed to get aboard a neutral ship with what he thought were impeccable documents. And now he was being taken into custody because some jumped-up travel agent had spotted that his suit bore no labels. It rankled that his fate had rested on something so apparently trivial.

Even then, the British naval officer was keen to reassure him: once the Swiss consul had confirmed that his passport was in order, Ernst Suse could rejoin the *Duca degli Abruzzi* and continue his journey to Naples. But the consul was never going to be consulted. When the boat reached the landing stage, a dozen armed soldiers were waiting. The sad little party of suspect passengers climbed on to the jetty and then the soldiers formed them up and they were marched through Gibraltar's streets to a small military police station high up on the Rock. The journey took over an hour through the hot, dusty town, then up into the barren landscape of this most vital of British possessions.

When Plüschow's turn came to be interviewed, he adopted the air of a man with a major grievance. Where was the Swiss consul? He had been promised that once his passport had been checked, then he could go. His captors smiled. They were used to 'Swiss' nationals making such demands. In fact it appeared that, since war had been declared, more Swiss citizens had passed through Gibraltar than there were living in Switzerland itself.

99

After the questioning came the physical search. Plüschow was third in line and an army sergeant motioned for him to raise his arms in order to be 'frisked'. The soldier ran his hands over Plüschow's arms and legs and then began on his upper torso. He stopped at the German's shirt pocket.

'Have you got any money?' he asked.

'No', said Plüschow.

The sergeant dipped his fingers into the pocket and triumphantly held up an American $20 gold coin.

Plüschow wrote later that his carelessness had given him away. In the same pocket he had slipped a tiny mother-of-pearl button that had come loose. Had he simply thrown it away, he said, then it would not have clinked against the coin. It is, however, difficult to imagine that anyone searching him thoroughly would not have discovered the coin anyway. A reasonably efficient search would also surely have given up what the sergeant found next: another gold coin and, most damning of all, a small Browning revolver.

Ernst Suse was now definitely not going to see the Swiss consul. Plüschow was told to dress and was then escorted to the prison yard where the rest of his fellow detainees from the *Duca degli Abruzzi* were already waiting to be taken to their quarters. Off they all trooped, to be given a rousing welcome by some fifty German civilian prisoners who had been interned at the beginning of the war. The civilians shared their food with the newcomers, and then Plüschow and the rest were set to work. They were paired off according to height, which meant that Plüschow had to share his duties with a desperate-looking character whom he had tried to avoid when they were marched off the *Duca degli Abruzzi*.

The work was hard – hauling sacks of coal and fetching water – and when evening came Plüschow was ready for his bunk, however uncomfortable it turned out to be. First, though, it was wash time and, to his dismay, he found himself again paired off with the filthy, unkempt character he had tried so hard to avoid. It was only then that Plüschow realized that the disgraceful state of the man was a disguise. He, too, was German. He had been running a motorcar dealership in America when war was declared and now, his business loose ends all tied up, he was trying to make his way home to serve the Fatherland in the military. Plüschow warmed to him and, with so much in common, they became good friends.

It had been quite a day. Plüschow had started it aboard the *Duca degli Abruzzi*, firmly believing that he was in the final stages of his long journey from China back to Germany. He ended it lying on a mattress that was as hard as stone, locked up in a military barracks atop the Rock of Gibraltar. What a way to spend his twenty-ninth birthday.

Sleep proved impossible and anyway, at 4am the barracks were roused by British non-commissioned officers who went through the rooms shouting and banging sticks. All German prisoners had to be ready to march off within twenty minutes. They would be sailing on the next boat for England.

Plüschow's heart sank and again he demanded to see the Swiss consul. But in his heart he must have known that, even if that were now possible, it was unlikely to help him. There was nothing for it but to comply – and comply with pride. As the prisoners from the *Duca degli Abruzzi* were marched down to the harbour, along with the German civilians who were also being moved, they burst into song with 'Die Wacht am Rhein'.

Their immediate destination was a large troopship, already overflowing with British military personnel. As the Germans boarded they were greeted with silence. No outward signs of animosity were displayed towards them. The most they were subjected to were a few sullen glares – and even the occasional look of pity. The men were led to the front portion of the cargo deck that had been petitioned off. There were hammocks in which to sleep, and a few tables and benches for their daytime needs. Not surprisingly, every porthole was tight shut. Two soldiers with fixed bayonets watched over them, while another two hovered on deck around the hatch. The prisoners were allowed on deck once a day, and if they wanted to use the

101

makeshift lavatory set up on the foredeck, they first had to ask a sentry for permission and were allowed up for that purpose only one at a time.

Plüschow might have wondered what adventure would befall him next. When the ship reached the Bay of Biscay, rough seas pitched and rolled the vessel for what seemed an eternity to the fifty-six men cooped up below, the majority of them suffering violent seasickness.

It must have occurred to them that there was also the threat of U-boats. Later that year, the troopship would certainly have been a target in what became a submarine-infested Mediterranean. Before February 1915, only ten British merchant ships had been lost to torpedoes; in August alone, forty-two British ships would be sunk. In the English Channel, however, the threat was already a very real one. As they neared their destination, the prisoners' time on deck was curtailed and Plüschow heard the sound of increasingly frequent lifeboat drills.

Ten days after leaving Gibraltar, the troopship docked at Plymouth and the prisoners were transferred to a train that would take them to Portsmouth. Ernst Suse was no more. He had been laid to rest on the voyage. Once he realized that the subterfuge was now pointless, Plüschow had announced his real identity. If nothing else, he thought that now the ship's captain knew he was an officer he might be transferred to first-class. And he might have been too, had he agreed to the captain's conditions that he would have to promise not to attempt to escape, and not to take any further part in the war. His refusal meant that he remained where he was, the only difference being that he was now watched even more closely.

It was the same on the journey along the South Coast. Plüschow was the only prisoner in his compartment. His fellow travellers were again armed soldiers and the conversation was muted to say the least. Plüschow was relieved when the train pulled into Portsmouth and he was reunited with the other detainees. They were formed up and marched through the gath-ering dusk to a nearby lock-up where a gaoler and two elderly soldiers, all of them more used to dealing with a few drunken sailors, must have scratched their heads at the arrival of fifty or more of the enemy.

The lock-up was certainly not equipped to deal with such a large number of inmates. There was no heat and the rooms were bare. To compound their misery, the prisoners had hardly eaten all day but that was resolved when the two old soldiers were bribed to fetch provisions. They returned with bread, butter, meat and tea, as well as wood. Soon Plüschow and the rest were enjoying a hearty supper by a roaring fire and later, he claimed, they even managed to obtain alcohol from the small canteen, thanks to the Masonic connections of one of his fellow prisoners.

Despite the spartan conditions that had greeted them when they arrived, thanks to their own ingenuity the inmates of this overflowing prison seem to have settled in quickly. And once fed and warmed through, not to mention relaxed by a few bottles of beer, they even managed to sleep well despite the tiny camp beds and thin straw-filled palliasses.

The following morning, a senior British officer arrived and Plüschow again made clear his true identity. The fact that he was a German officer entitled him to treatment as a prisoner of war rather than the rag-tag status that he currently endured. The British officer appeared amenable enough but Plüschow felt that he would promise just about anything in order to move the problem along and out of his own jurisdiction. A day later that was exactly what happened. The prisoners were marched back down to the harbour and on to a small steamer that chugged out into the Solent until it reached a liner (either the Allan Line's RMS *Tunisian* or the Dominion Line's SS *Canada*) that was being used as a prison ship off Ryde on the Isle of Wight. Negotiation were opened but the officer in charge refused to take them and the steamer was sent on its way again.

The same scene was re-enacted on the Cunard liner *Andania* which had been put into service as a troopship on the outbreak of war but which was now also being used as a makeshift prison. This time, however, after a heated argument between the two

British officers, the Germans were taken on board. The *Andania* had been launched in 1913, one of three ships Cunard built expressly for the Canadian trade route. She would meet a tragic end. Released from duty in March 1916, she was put on the London–New York route that May, and in January 1918 was attacked by a U-boat off the Irish coast and sunk. For now, though, she was to be Gunther Plüschow's latest home.

Again he demanded to be taken to an officers' camp but the new man in charge – according to Plüschow 'a fat, bumptious Englishman' who had bought his commission with money he had made before the war as a commercial traveller for a whisky distilling company – did not even bother to pretend that he cared. Plüschow said that the officer claimed to have had heard all about the man who fled from Tsingtao and who had escaped several times. Far from being treated like an officer, he would be locked up and put on short rations in retaliation for the way English officers were being treated in German POW camps. Once again, we have to remind ourselves that Plüschow was writing this account for publication in wartime Germany, in 1916. That is not to suggest that the conversation did not take place but simply to point out that if he exaggerated the point, who could blame him?

Plüschow also described conditions aboard the *Andania*, which now accommodated about 1,000 prisoners, all of whom were kept below decks with little opportunity for exercise. As this was still very early in the conflict, it comes as no surprise. When it came to housing prisoners, the war had caught all governments on the hop and they were unprepared – and probably unconcerned since everyone thought that the war would be over fairly quickly – about what to do with captured soldiers and sailors, never mind all the enemy aliens in their respective civilian populations. In late September 1914, of the 13,600 internees held in Britain, only 3,100 had been captured in battle; the remainder were from the German community living in the country when war broke out.

There were precious few regulations about the treatment of prisoners, military or civilian. And the ones that were laid down, by the Hague Conference of 1907, were ambiguous. Each power had to compile records of each prisoner it held, for the information of relatives. Also, prisoners of war were not to be used for war work but that was ignored in some countries later in the war when they were presented with a shortage of labour. Britain's only other guideline seems to have been a Royal Warrant for the Maintenance of Discipline, dated 3 August 1914; in the main that was concerned with the punishments that could be meted out to prisoners who broke the rules.

Prison camps were hastily organized in buildings such as ancestral homes, on islands, at army camps, on racecourses like Newbury – and on nine transatlantic liners like the *Andania*, which were requisitioned at a cost of between £7,000 and £12,000 per month, depending on tonnage.

Initially all camps were run by a department of the Adjutant-General's Office that reported directly to the War Office and was known simply as 'AG3'. In February 1915, the Directorate of Prisoners of War, under Lieutenant General Sir Herbert Eversley Belfield (who had been in charge of AG3), came into being, also under the War Office. Even then it was devoted mostly to civilians and merchant seamen whose vessels had been captured. The number of captured German military was few in number until the end of 1917, one of the few notable hauls before that being the 348 naval prisoners taken at the Battle of the Heligoland Bight on 28 August 1914.

If any German prisoners had complaints about their treatment, they did not take advantage of an inspection visit by two members of the International Red Cross who toured POW camps in Britain in February 1915 – the very month that Gunther Plüschow arrived – and reported no cases of dissatisfaction. That concurred with the findings of John B Jackson, a member of the US Embassy in Berlin acting on behalf of the German government, who was allowed to make unannounced visits to British camps in the winter of 1914–15 and, having visited thirteen camps and all nine ships, found the only complaints came from civilians who had been taken from neutral ships or from the colonies and who were aggrieved about the manner of their detention rather than their subsequent living conditions.

Gunther Plüschow, however, had plenty of complaints about the conditions on board the *Andania*, although he admitted that once he had befriended a British non-commissioned officer he was allowed to use a small cabin 'which even boasted of a port-hole'. For all that, life was monotonous. Reveille was at 6am, lights out at 10pm. Each morning and afternoon the prisoners had to stand-to on the upper deck for about two hours, and roll call was at noon. They ate, twelve to a table, in a cavernous dining room and each man, Plüschow included, had to take his turn at fetching and serving the food, and washing up.

Plüschow also told a story about the officer in charge of the *Andania* prison ship who, he said, offered the prisoners a separate dining area, better food and the opportunity to be excused washing up. All they had to do was to pay him 2.50 marks a day; Plüschow said that the Germans were enraged by this 'rank swindle' and refused. Plüschow applied in writing to be trans-ferred to an officers' prison but he had to channel it through his nemesis, who of course did not pass it on. Instead he told Plüschow that he would have to pay 'for our English officers forced to drag ploughs over fields'. According to Plüschow, he began to mock the prisoners. 'What, still here?' he would ask at lights out.

Soon open rebellion threatened. The civilian prisoners were ordered to scrub the first-class deck and scour the portholes. They refused, so everyone was deprived of their dinner and forced to bed at 9pm. The officer in charge – 'temporary lieu-tenant and temporary gentleman' Plüschow called him – blamed the flying man from Tsingtao for all the problems. He was the ringleader.

The following day, however, Plüschow and the whisky-salesmen turned prison governor parted company. A steamer pulled alongside the *Andania* and Plüschow and some of his colleagues, about thirty in number, were taken off the ship and put ashore, from where they were taken to a railway station. The following month, the War Office dispensed with all three prison ships moored off Ryde, although it retained the ones at Gosport and Southend.

Plüschow, meanwhile, was travelling west, to Dorchester, the county town of Dorset. Again in his memoirs he underlines that he was considered an important prisoner, travelling in his own compartment, accompanied this time not only by three non-commissioned officers but also by an officer. It was evening by the time the train pulled into the small country town of some 9,000 inhabitants, and Plüschow was agreeably surprised by his welcome.

A Captain Mitchell asked him whether he was an officer.

'Yes, I am', Plüschow replied.

'In that case', said Captain Mitchell, 'I'm surprised that you've been sent here. This is a camp for soldiers.'

The captain apologized for not having another officer available to escort Plüschow and asked if he minded going with the senior NCO instead. And of course, he must walk alone, not with the other prisoners. And so Lieutenant Plüschow made his way through the streets of the town made famous by Thomas Hardy, towards his latest place of incarceration. He had gone only a few yards when, around the corner, came about fifty German ordinary soldiers, commandeered from the camp to collect the incoming prisoners' luggage from the station.

Plüschow was taken aback by the behaviour of the local civilian population who stood and watched in silence as the procession marched past. Occasionally a house curtain twitched. Plüschow even thought that the locals might be enjoying the German drinking and military songs that the soldiers were singing as they made their way past.

Dorchester POW camp had opened in August 1914, a hastily converted army camp that initially held only civilian internees and those captured at sea. The first military prisoners had arrived there on 27 August, and by 1915 the number held had risen to around 2,000, including 450 internees transferred from the Isle of Man. Plüschow was shown to a small wooden hut that held about thirty men. There were no beds, just small straw mattresses that lay on the floor, and two blankets each. Again, Captain Mitchell apologized and hoped that Lieutenant Plüschow would forgive the lack of proper facilities for an officer.

The new guest did not complain. In fact, he wrote later, the food was good (and there was plenty of it) and the treatment handed out by his captors was beyond reproach. Both Mitchell and his commanding officer, Major Owen, were regular soldiers who had seen action. The medical officer was keen to see that the prisoners were given ample opportunities for sport, while the senior German prisoner, a warrant officer who had been a merchant in Munich before the war, spoke fluent English and was the perfect go-between. In fact, Plüschow mused, he did not know what the British would have done without the NCO, who seemed to be in total charge of organizing his fellow prisoners.

Despite the relative comfort of Dorchester, Plüschow still wanted to be moved to an officers' camp, and since his previous request had never got past the dreadful officer in charge of the *Andania*, he wrote out another application and presented it to Major Owen. This time it was passed on through the appropriate channels, but two weeks went by before Plüschow received a reply. His heart sank a little because he was asked if he could provide the name of someone in England to vouch for him. He was not keen to involve an acquaintance that he had made before the war, when things were so different, but he had no choice.

While he was waiting to learn if his request had now been accepted, the civilian prisoners were moved out of Dorchester. Plüschow was concerned that he too might be transferred and that his own move to officers' quarters might be delayed still further. He sought out Major Owen and asked to be allowed to remain in the soldiers' camp while his request was sorted out. The major had no objection. Indeed, he arranged for Plüschow to leave the now empty hut and be billeted instead in a small room over some stables.

There Plüschow found a warm welcome among men who had been captured in September 1914, during what would later be known as the First Battle of the Marne that set the stage for four years of stalemate on the Western Front. He later recalled his new roommates: a huge Bavarian infantryman who was known to one and all as 'Schorsch' and who had been elected the room's cook; a Hussars private from Lorraine who had been a policeman before the war; and two riflemen from the Frisian Islands. About a week after Plüschow arrived, they received another officer, a sub-lieutenant who had been fished out of the North Sea when the airship in which he was the observer was downed.

Plüschow enjoyed their company immensely. He particularly enjoyed hearing of their experiences. His own brief war had been fought many thousands of miles from the European theatre and, after he had eagerly lapped up stories of the fighting in France and Belgium, he related tales of his own one-man aerial war in the skies over Tsingtao.

The camp's medical officer was still anxious that all prisoners should get regular exercise and each afternoon several hundred of them were taken on walks around the camp and even allowed into the countryside beyond. This generally involved marching through the town and the Germans gave full vent to songs like 'Die Wacht am Rhein' and 'Deutschland Hoch in Ehren' (Germany High in Honours). Again, Plüschow was surprised to see that the locals expressed no anger whatsoever towards the German soldiers.

Plüschow learned that Major Owen and Captain Mitchell had even insisted that their own wives visit the camp to see for themselves that Germans were not the barbarians they had been portrayed as in British newspapers. When the wives arrived, they were apparently serenaded by the prisoners' choir, which moved the women to tears. Clearly, life at Dorchester camp moved along in a civilized fashion.

Towards the end of March, Plüschow received his first letter from home in nine months. It contained devastating news: in October 1914 Carlotta, his 'beloved little sister', had died in Wismar, aged 23. Hans (in the infantry) and Wolfgang (like Gunther, an airman) were apparently safe, despite both being on active service, but the loss of his 'best friend' must have affected him deeply.

At about the same time, he received some good news. At last he was to be transferred to an officers' camp. He said his good-byes to the soldiers with whom he had formed a short but intense bond, and after collecting his belongings – few in number but including the hockey stick that his captors had provided – he was marched back to Dorchester railway station. Major Owen came with him to see him off, a gesture that Plüschow greatly appreciated. In some ways he was sorry to leave Dorchester. (In the 1930s former German prisoners of war who had been held at Dorchester returned to pay their respects to the forty-eight comrades who had died at the camp, almost all from natural causes, and who were buried in Dorchester's Fordington cemetery. The former inmates, who stayed in the homes of people who had once guarded them, gave the Nazi salute over the graves. After the Second World War the remains were removed to Germany.)

In May 1915, just over a month after Plüschow had left, the camp became the subject of a controversy when a Major Bruno Schmidt-Reder published a booklet in Germany, detailing his release from Dorchester after being diagnosed with a serious ear condition. In the House of Commons, the Under-Secretary of State for War, the Scottish Liberal Harold Tennant, was asked by Ulsterman Ronald McNeill, the Tory MP for East Kent, if he thought it acceptable that an enemy prisoner of war should be released without having to give an undertaking that he would not bear arms again. Not only that, there had apparently been no British officer in the camp on the day of Schmidt-Reder's release. Perhaps worst of all, the booklet contained photographs of the camp, presumably taken by the prisoner. Tennant replied: 'Photographs of the camp, I should have thought, would have been harmless. Of course, if he had other photographs, it might be dangerous to let him return, but I am not aware that he had any photographs.'

～

After a train journey of several hours, Plüschow arrived in Maidenhead, 25 miles west of London, and greatly appreciated another gesture: the gold coins that had been taken from the pockets of Ernst Suse, the Swiss locksmith, back in Gibraltar were returned to Gunther Plüschow. Plüschow reflected on the honesty of the English; the coins had obviously been properly transferred every time he was moved. He was, though, surprised that they had survived the *Andania* and its dreadful commandant.

A motor car took him on the last few miles of his journey: to the officers' camp at Holyport, housed in a late Victorian walled mansion that had replaced a splendid black and white timber-framed sixteenth-century manor house, once the home of Nell Gwynne, the mistress of Charles II. The camp had been opened early in the war and by 1915 it held 100 German officers and 40 other ranks that acted as their orderlies. As his transport reached the main gates, the sentries presented arms and then Plüschow was whisked through to what was almost a home from home.

There were faces that he had last seen at Tsingtao, including the victors of the Battle of Coronel the previous November, and a few of those who had survived the German defeat at the Battle of the Falkland Islands in December. According to the *Washington Post* these included the German commandant at Holyport 'who acts as the sole intermediary between the prisoners and the British commandant'. He was, said the newspaper, a man named 'Captain Bochhamer, commander of the German cruiser *Gneisenau*, sunk in the battle off the Falklands'. Of course, the *Gneisenau*'s actual captain, Julius Maerker, had been lost with his ship during Falklands engagement.

There was much catching up to be done but first the new man had to be shown to his quarters, where there was yet another pleasant surprise waiting for him. His billet held eight men – and each of them had a proper bed. There were even clean white sheets. After two months of trying to sleep on palliasses placed on hard floors, Plüschow could only regard what he saw as an absolute luxury.

Life at Holyport just got better. The food was good if not exactly to German tastes, and two German chefs from trans-atlantic liners supervised the preparation of meals. The prisoners were allowed wine and light beer, but no whisky, and there were several messes as well as reading and dining rooms. The commandant was a decent individual, and the prisoners were allowed to move around the grounds freely until lights out at 10pm. There were football and hockey pitches, a fortnightly visit from a tailor and a general clothier, and a regular delivery of post from Germany.

Of course, there were the ever-present reminders that this was still a prison – the sentries, the barbed wire entanglements and the fences that were brilliantly floodlit during the hours of dark-ness – but letters and parcels took just over a week to arrive from home, and the officers received money from the German govern-ment, of which half was retained for their keep, the rest they could spend as they wished in the camp canteen, or in renewing their wardrobes.

Plüschow soon discovered that his fellow prisoners were a fascinating bunch. The world-renowned geologist Ferdinand Friedensburg, who had been a consulting engineer on the Panama Canal that had finally opened in 1914, had been also been taken at Gibraltar on a journey back from the United States, in his case to take up a commission in the 2nd Silesian Field Artillery. An escape attempt resulted in him breaking both legs and in December 1914 he was transferred to Holyport where he gave lectures to fellow prisoners. From 1946 to 1951 Friedensburg would serve as the deputy mayor of Greater Berlin, taking over during the Soviet blockade of the city when the mayor fell ill.

Astronomer Dr Arnold Kohlschütter, who had been working at the solar observatory at Mount Wilson in California, had been taken from the Italian liner *Ancona* at Gibraltar after being recalled to serve as a reserve in the German Army. He was more fortunate than many: in November 1915, the *Ancona*, working the popular New York–Naples run, would be sunk by an Austrian U-boat with the loss of more than 200 lives; coming only six months after the sinking of the *Lusitania*, it further enraged American opinion. Kohlschütter, meanwhile, would one day have a crater on the moon named after him.

George Millington-Herrman, son of a high-ranking official of the Deutsche Bank in Berlin and himself connected with the bank's New York branch, had been on his way back to home to serve as a lieutenant in the *Landwehr* (reserve) cavalry when the British interrupted his journey.

Paul Lutz, a former surgeon for the Norddeutscher Lloyd liner *Kronprinzessian Cecille*, had been captured at Falmouth. Initially held at Dartford's Lower Southern Hospital which had become a war hospital for seriously injured German prisoners, he now taught Spanish to the prisoners at Holyport, 'preparatory to a German commercial invasion of Latin America after the war', according to the *Washington Post*. Other civilian internees included Baron Egon von Rechenberg, attaché to the German Consul General in New York; on his way back to Germany, von Rechenberg had been removed from the Italian liner SS *America* at Gibraltar. Carl Bötefür, Germany's Director of Customs in the Cameroons, was also held at Holyport before he was repatriated.

Captain Mühlbauer was in command of an East African trading vessel when the war broke out: 'We had no wireless and knew nothing of the war. My ship arrived at Gibraltar from Malta and, before I knew it, I was a British prisoner.'

Victor von Borosini Schoenstadt, a social worker attached to the Hull House project in Chicago, was on holiday in Saxony when war broke out. He joined the army as a first lieutenant and was captured in November 1914, during what would become known as the First Battle of Ypres. His American wife had been to England to visit him and he wanted to know: 'Was Carter Harrison re-elected mayor of Chicago? And did they ever do anything about the subway?'

Later in 1915, Dr Martin Luther, who had served as surgeon

on the ill-fated *Emden* and who was a descendant of history's greatest reformer, would be a prisoner at Holyport. An eye-witness described him as being little more than a nervous wreck when he was captured, having spent twenty-four hours on the battered ship, with many wounded under his care but with none of his staff remaining and very few dressings or other medical equipment.

Many captured medical officers, both civilian and army and naval, ended up at Holyport, including Dr Ernst Strauss, who had been taken prisoner when the Royal Navy controversially seized the German hospital ship *Ophelia* in October 1914, claiming that she had been 'adapted and used as a signalling ship for military purposes'. In May 1915, a British court convicted the *Ophelia* of carrying signalling equipment (lamps and rockets) without adequate justification, and of throwing documents over-board and sending a coded message to the military station at Nordeich just before being boarded in the North Sea. The court ruled that the ship was a lawful prize of war. One of Strauss's colleagues from the *Ophelia*, a Dr Pfeiffer, was stripped of his medical status after being sent to Holyport.

In December 1915, the *New York Times* would give a fascinating insight into life at Holyport, albeit one that borrowed the history of the previous building:

> Ensconced in a turreted house built in the seventeenth century by Charles II, for his favourite, Nell Glynn [*sic*], in the midst of a lordly environment at Holyport, near Maidenhead, are 125 German officers, as prisoners of war. The New York Times correspondent went to this camp yesterday on the first trip of American newspaper corre-spondents to any German officers' camp in England . . .
> One striking things about this German camp is that nearly all the prisoners speak English well and those who did not

understand it when they were taken are now acquiring it under the tutelage of others. They are a proud but restive lot, these captives. The British Government allows them to wear the uniforms of their own regiments and they are permitted to indulge in luxuries. They have the range of the capricious walled grounds to stroll in, and have German body servants and German cooks.

As showing how eager they are to get away, it was said yesterday that recently a futile attempt was undertaken to escape. It was the only one made so far and was discovered by the commandant . . .

The correspondent asked several of the officers how they liked prison life and invariably the reply was that although they were handsomely treated by the British, they were eager to get back into the fight. They have been in the camp so long – many of them nearly a year – that the monotony is becoming deadly. When the correspondent reached the camp, and passed through the gate of the thick barbed-wire entanglements just inside the walls, the officers were emerging from the house for their daily athletics in the field.

They strode past with eyes turned to salute and bounded into the field. They wore the uniforms of the Prussian guard and the Jäger guard, the Kaiser's crack regiments, and many others. There were also twenty naval men among the group.

While the men were in the field, the newspaper correspondents were taken into their quarters in the Nell Gwynne castle. The officers are grouped in it according to their own tastes, going into cliques. So clannish are these cliques that the commissioned officers will not fraternize with what are called 'rankers', or those who have won promotion in the field. The officers stick to their own sets, and although they are all in one house, they make up distinct communities having little to do with each other.

One evidence of their loftiness is the attitude of the army officers towards the naval officers, the former holding aloof and saying that while the army has done its work, the navy has failed to do anything. This naturally nettles the naval officers. A dozen officers as a rule are allowed a large room. Some have tapestries on the walls and some extra rugs on the floors, most of the officers having means of their own. Over the bed of one officer was a large print of the Kaiser, while others have various German reminders, including photographs of the Crown Prince.

One thing the British Government makes no effort to do in these military camps is to force the men to sink their national sentiment. They are even allowed to sing German songs. In this camp is a chorus of a dozen Heidelberg men who lead every night in singing favourite German songs, and they are never molested . . .

None of the officers spoke one word about the war . . . the prisoners get from $1 a day for officers of the lowest rank up to $5 a day for physicians. They are permitted their own bill of fare, which their own chef prepares, also beer and wine. They are allowed to see visitors once a month and to receive letters . . . but these are censored. The prisoners are getting Christmas parcels this week. A picturesque sight was a tiny Christmas tree of tinsel in nearly every room while holly was festooned on the walls.

Gunther Plüschow would not be there by Christmas, but of Holyport he later wrote: 'In the beginning, I thought myself in Paradise.'

Chapter 13

Welcome to Donington Hall

One evening towards the end of April 1915, the gentle existence enjoyed by Gunther Plüschow and his fellow inmates at Holyport was rudely interrupted when an order was received from the Directorate of Prisoners of War to transfer fifty officers to a new prisoner of war camp for officers that had recently been established at Castle Donington, a small town on the Leicestershire–Derbyshire border. No one wanted to leave Holyport but, of course, they had no choice. On Saturday, 1 May, only a month after he had arrived at Maidenhead railway station, Plüschow, along with his colleagues, was driven back there and ushered into one of two carriages reserved for the prisoners who were being transferred. Eventually, after the compartments had been made secure and guards posted, the train eased its way out of the station and headed north as a heat haze rose from the Berkshire fields.

In 1915, Castle Donington in north-west Leicestershire was home to some 6,000 souls (it isn't much bigger in 2009). It stood on the old Nottingham–Birmingham trunk road, a pleasant little town with its share of Georgian and Regency buildings. Several timber-framed houses, dating from the seventeenth century and earlier, lined the main road, but, despite its name, there was no longer a castle. The first had been levelled by King John's troops in 1216 – a year earlier, the castle's owner had been a signatory to Magna Carta – and the second was demolished at the end of the sixteenth century. Some of its stone had been used to build the first Donington Hall, home to members of the Hastings family from 1595 until the death of Lord Donington in 1895, by which time there was a new hall. In 1793, Earl Moira, later 1st

Marquis Hastings, had replaced the old hall with one built in the 'Strawberry Hill Gothic' style first made fashionable by Horace Walpole. A tall vaulted porch surmounted the main entrance and the Gothic theme continued in the vaulted entrance hall where a fireplace still carried the Hastings insignia. Beyond was a splendid oval stairway. In 2008, Donington Hall was the head-quarters of British Midland Airways, in which the German airline, Lufthansa, had recently acquired a controlling interest. In May 1915, it was to be the new, if temporary, home of a German aviator called Gunther Plüschow.

Plüschow was the only naval officer to be moved from Holyport but he did have the company of another flying man, his close friend Fritz Siebel, an army officer. As their train steamed north, both men wondered what their new camp would be like. Occasionally, when the train stopped at a station, locals peering through the carriage window interrupted their thoughts. Most were simply curious and content to stare but, on one occasion, an old woman stuck out her tongue. For some reason, Plüschow thought that she might have been a Suffragette. Certainly, five months later, the Women's Social and Political Union, the leading militant organization campaigning for women's suffrage in the United Kingdom, changed its newspaper's title from *The Suffragette* to *Britannia*, its patriotic view of the war reflected in its new slogan: 'For King, For Country, For Freedom'. Plüschow was certainly aware of what was happening politically in his captors' country.

At last, late in the afternoon of that scorching May Day, the train pulled into Castle Donington station, on a branch line of the Midland Railway. Plüschow makes no mention of them having to change trains on the journey and so, as it seems highly unlikely that there would have been a scheduled service between Maidstone and Castle Donington, this one was probably specially chartered, or at least the carriages carrying the Germans were switched to another train.

The prisoners were quickly detrained and told to fall in. Then, guarded by about sixty soldiers of the Leicestershire Regiment armed with rifles and with bayonets fixed, they were ordered to 'Quick march'. Outside the station they were left with no illusions that, if the inquisitive bystanders at other stations had been content to stand and stare, or at most make rude faces, locals at Castle Donington were in a far more belligerent mood. Women and children – there were hardly any men present – booed and whistled, ran alongside the column of prisoners, and occasionally hurled stones and clods of earth at them. Plüschow remarked later that some of his comrades had become accustomed to this in France but that it was a new experience for them to see the British 'lower orders', as he put it, behaving in this way.

Then the scene descended into chaos. First a car appeared, driven by the army lieutenant who would be acting as an interpreter for the prisoners – 'a fat and supercilious individual' when they got to know him, according to Plüschow – and in his haste to make something of an impression, he drove into one of the guards. The British soldier was lifted clear by two Germans and the women momentarily turned their spleen towards the officer, who drove away at high speed. The women then returned to their original objective of pelting the prisoners and the situation was threatening to get out of hand when around the corner came a small herd of cows. The women abandoned their mission, gathered up their skirts, grabbed their children and fled. Some fell, others tripped over them, and both German prisoners and their British guards stood roaring with laughter at the confusion as women lay kicking and screaming on the road and in the ditches either side of it. Welcome to Castle Donington.

Ignoring the women, the cows ambled slowly on their way and eventually, in the opposite direction, fifty German prisoners of war, together with their escorts, marched briskly on theirs. There was no shade and the late afternoon sun burned down on the column as it made its way from the station towards Donington Hall, which stood in its own parkland some 2 miles away. Plüschow decided to spend the journey trying to memorize landmarks that might come in useful later. Eventually, the Hall came into sight. Leased to the War Office by the brewer Frederick Gratton, son of Lord Gratton of Stapleford Park, Leicestershire, who had purchased the estate in 1901, the house was surrounded by two high wire fences, an electrified wire running around each of them, and complicated wire entanglements in between. There was an outer guardhouse overlooking the main road. Around a hundred officers, as Plüschow would soon discover, were housed in the main house; their servants – some fifty German military orderlies – were quartered in wooden huts. The camp had come into existence at the start of 1915 and had soon attracted the attention of both the House of Commons and the press.

On 23 February that year, in a report headed 'Luxury For Prisoners', the *New York Times* said:

Nearly $100,000, it was disclosed in today's Parliamentary paper, has been expended by the British Government in fitting up Donington Hall in Leicestershire for the use of German officers in England as prisoners of war. About twenty thousand dollars was expended for furniture alone. The Government has been criticized for such lavish treatment of German prisoners.

Donington is one of the finest mansions in the Midlands. It stands in splendid grounds on the banks of the Trent. The ground floor of the building has been converted into a clubhouse and numerous bathrooms have been installed.

In London, the *Daily Mail* told its readers:

The house is finely appointed with carved oak panels and a carved and polished elm ceiling, a smoking lounge equal to that of a good hotel, six bathrooms with hot and cold water and a shower bath; and also a medical ward with doctors and attendants. Electric light has been installed and all the compartments are heated.

There is also a canteen from which the prisoners can obtain wines and spirits of all the principal brands. They will be waited on by German valets, shaved by German barbers and served with food by German waiters, captured in the German ranks.

The newspaper added: 'One must suppose that the War Office has really at heart the idea of reforming the Prussian officers, and by letting them soak in the suggestion of beauty and peace, showing them the difference between the *kultur* that watched Louvain burn and the culture inspired by a sunset in the valley of the Trent.'

The *Staffordshire Sentinel*, meanwhile, told its readers that so many packages for the prisoners at Donington Hall had been received from Germany that 'the village post office has been obliged to enlarge its staff'.

In March, John Butcher, MP for York, asked the Under-Secretary of State for War, Harold Tennant, whether

in view of the fact that many of our wounded officers and men at home are housed in places not so commodious and not so well equipped with all modern appliances and comforts as Donington Hall, he would transfer the German officers and their servants now occupying Donington Hall to other quarters and give directions that in future Donington Hall should be occupied by wounded officers and men belonging to our own army or those of our allies?

The Under-Secretary was quick to repudiate the suggestion that German prisoners were better treated than Allied wounded.

Later in 1915, in an article alleging German ill treatment of British prisoners of war, Sir Arthur Conan Doyle would write:

What makes it so odious is that it is a method to which we can make no reply. It is true that we have very many Germans, officers and civilians, in our power. The total number of Germans on whom we could lay our hands is far higher than the total number of British in Germany. Among

121

them is the son of the chief murderer, at present leading a life of ease at Donington Hall.

In the still-neutral United States, however, another picture was painted by the *Washington Post*, which, in April 1915, reported:

> True, it is a very beautiful and picturesque country seat, standing in a magnificent park. But, like the Duke of Sutherland's magnificent palace of Trentham Hall nearby, it has been rendered unpleasant by the noisome smell from the River Trent which runs through both properties and which has been literally poisoned by the potteries and factories of one kind or another situated on its banks.

In fact, Trentham Hall was near Stoke-on-Trent, and whether waste from the Staffordshire potteries bothered the inmates of Donington Hall, 41 miles away, is not recorded. The camp was certainly already well-known and would maintain its reputation throughout the war. In 1917, the satirical magazine *Punch* would publish an article entitled 'The Mudlarks' in which it reported:

> Patrick and his friends attacked in a snowstorm, dropped into a German post, gave the occupants every assistance in evacuating, and prepared to make themselves at home. While they were clearing up the mess, they found they had taken a prisoner, a blond Bavarian hero who had found it impossible to leave with his friends on account of half-a-ton of sandbags on his chest. They excavated him, told him if he was a good boy they'd give him a ticket to Donington Hall at nightfall, christened him Goldilocks for the time being, and threw him some rations, among which was a tin of butter.

Under the headline 'Our Pampered Conchies', the same magazine, referring to an article in *The Times* which, slightly misleadingly, reported that 'there was a long and interesting debate on the imprisonment of conscientious objectors in the House of Lords', added its own comment: 'This beats Donington Hall to a frazzle.'

Plüschow was already aware of the publicity surrounding the apparent luxury of Donington Hall. He wrote later that, for all he had read about the camp, 'it should have been Paradise'. There were even rumours that fox hunts were arranged especially for the benefit of the prisoners. That was untrue, of course, but on 1 May 1915, Gunther Plüschow was certainly impressed by the initial welcome he and his fellow prisoners found there. To greet them was a full turnout of the guard, which presented arms while the officer in command of the guard, and the two lieutenants accompanying him, all saluted. The German officers were then 'received' – Plüschow's own description – by the camp commandant before being shown to their rooms. It sounds almost like the arrival of a shooting party for a country house weekend.

Plüschow was to share a room with four colleagues, one of whom, he was pleased to note, was his old friend, Fritz Siebel. Indeed, there were many old faces in the camp, including several flying men from both the army and navy. Some of the prisoners had been picked up from the sea after their vessels had been sunk; they included some of the 260 survivors of the armoured cruiser *Blüche*, which had been lost during the Battle of Dogger Bank on 24 January 1915.

Plüschow was less pleased to discover that, far from the prisoners' quarters being lavishly furnished as rumoured, their rooms were bare. 'There was no trace of . . . entertainment rooms or hunting', he noted later. In fact, for some time Donington Hall had been devoid of virtually all the contents that had once made it such a prime example of the English country house. The plain truth was that the house and estate were impoverished and a drain on its current owner, who had never occupied it. Those who repeated stories of its luxurious state were thinking of another, grander age. True, a photograph released in 1918 showed a prisoner's room at Donington Hall equipped with a chest of drawers in use as a dressing table with an attractive cover and flowers, an armchair, and plenty of books and pictures. As it was taken on behalf of the Central Prisoners of War Committee of the British Red Cross and Order of St John, one must assume that it was a genuine representation of officer prisoners' accommodation there, at least by the end of the war.

After the men had arrived from Holyport, there were around 120 prisoners incarcerated at Donington Hall and, by June 1916, the camp would house 141 officers, 51 orderlies and 3 civilians, all Germans save for 4 Austrian army officers and a lone Turkish naval officer. In May 1915 Plüschow claimed that he and his colleagues were 'packed together like pickled herrings', and he shuddered to think what conditions would have been like had the 'advertized' full complement of 400 to 500 officers been present. The mess, kitchens and bathrooms were far from sufficient for even half that number. Plüschow did not mind the English food, although it was not to everyone's taste. A sample menu was cereal, bread and marmalade, and tea for breakfast; soup, cold meat and baked potato for lunch; and roast mutton, potatoes, cabbage and jam pancake for dinner. The prisoners could indeed purchase wine (officers in POW camps still received their pay from Germany) but whether the choice and quality was as grand as some newspapers claimed is, again, not recorded.

Plüschow was also happy enough with the camp commandant, Lieutenant Colonel Francis Slater Picot, who, although he was inclined to remind everyone of his authority, nevertheless took it upon himself to make the prisoners' life as tolerable as possible, taking a special interest in their sports. Australian-born Picot was 55 years old. Formerly of the Wiltshire Regiment, for some years he had been in charge of a military prison with the rank of major. In October 1914, Picot had been brought out of retirement, promoted to temporary lieutenant colonel and returned to duty as commandant of a hastily organized POW camp at Frith Hill in Surrey. At the beginning of 1915 he took over at the newly opened Donington Hall camp. A week before Plüschow arrived there, Picot's son, Philip Simons Picot, a mining engineer who had returned from Malaya on the outbreak of war to be commissioned in the Sherwood Foresters, had sailed for Gallipoli. Two months later, on 11 July 1915, Philip Simons Picot, now attached to the Royal Scots Fusiliers, would be killed in action. It was a tragedy that would have saddened Plüschow who regarded his father as 'a distinguished, intelligent man, and a perfect soldier'.

Apart from Lieutenant Colonel Picot, the only redeeming feature of Donington Hall, so far as its prisoners were concerned, was the park in which it stood. A deer park that dated back to the twelfth century, and which was relandscaped by Humphrey Repton, the last great English landscape designer of the eighteenth century, in 1915 Donington Park still contained herds of deer that wandered among its mighty oaks and it still retained the essential timelessness of centuries past. Sixteen years later that would all change when one Fred Craner, an energetic official of the Derby and District Motor Club, would persuade the Donington estate's new owner, John Gillies Shields – who had been land agent to the late Lord Donington – to allow motor cycle racing there. In 1933, motor car racing was first staged on a circuit that utilized the park's old tracks and pathways, on which tarmac had been laid, and Donington Park motor racing circuit was born. In 1935 it staged the first-ever Grand Prix to be held on a road track in Britain. On 22 October 1938, with Britain and Germany on the brink of another war, 60,000 British motor racing fans marvelled at the German racing cars fielded by Mercedes-Benz and Auto Union – and funded by Adolf Hitler – when Donington Park played host to a Grand Prix delayed by Germany's designs on Czechoslovakia and its subsequent occupation of the Sudetenland which followed the Munich agreement.

All this, of course, was far into the future, and certainly unimaginable in the early summer of 1915 as Gunther Plüschow took stock of his new surroundings. The camp was divided into two zones – effectively night and day areas – that were marked by those high barbed-wire fences and illuminated at night by powerful arc lamps. Night and day, sentries patrolled the whole area.

Despite all this, the main benefit of the park to the prisoners was that it allowed for greater movement than at Holyport and, as well as the provision of three tennis courts, there was room to play hockey and football. At 6pm each evening, however, after the day's main roll call, the park was closed to the prisoners, who then had nothing much to do except read that day's newspapers – they were allowed *The Times* and the *Morning Post* – which naturally viewed the war from a very different angle to that of Donington Hall's involuntary guests. For them it was depressing to read about the war only from the British side and even though they could convince themselves that most of the reports were probably propaganda, it was still wearing on the prisoners' spirits to read nothing but bad things about Germany – how their country was suffering defeat on the battlefield, and famine and even revolution on the home front.

Just one week after Plüschow's arrival, however, those newspapers reported a major tragedy, the bare facts of which could not be disputed, even though there were later conspiracy theories as to how it had been allowed to happen. On 7 May, off the south-west coast of Ireland, the 32,000-ton Cunard liner RMS *Lusitania*, en route from New York, was torpedoed by the German U-boat *U20*. The ship took only eighteen minutes to sink, taking with her 1,198 passengers and crew. The newspapers were unanimous in their verdict: this was not an act of war; it was a war crime, final proof to anyone who still doubted tales of German brutality. Considering the reception they had received at Castle Donington station before the sinking of the *Lusitania*, perhaps behind the double barbed-wire fences of Donington Hall was now the safest place for a German after all.

Chapter 14

How Far is Derby?

Safe haven or not, the main problem at Donington Hall, indeed at any prison camp, was boredom. Several of those held there suffered from what became known as 'barbed wire psychosis', a loss of contact with reality that impaired their daily functioning, and many devised ways to combat the tedium of captivity. Education courses and the formation of small musical groups helped, while some spent their time making objects for sale or display. In a letter home, one officer held at Donington Hall told his wife: 'We have a continuous display of things we have made, including oil-paintings, pastels, engine construction and carving work.'

But, for some, captivity was becoming an unbearable mental load and Gunther Plüschow was one who suffered most. Even the fact that letters and parcels from his family were still being delivered, even the companionship of his fellow officers, could do nothing to ease the feeling of intense loneliness, homesickness – and the sheer hopelessness of his situation. He was a man of action, always had been. Games of hockey might be diverting for an hour or two, but they were no substitute for flying, which was what he missed most. He would lie on the grass, hands behind his head, gazing up into the sky and wish with all his heart that he could be up there. And occasionally, just to add to his pain, a British aircraft would soar across the self-same sky. At moments like that, how the hero of Tsingtao envied the pilot in his flying machine. Then his spirits sank even lower.

Plüschow knew that he was behaving badly towards his comrades, so taut had his nerves become. He tried to pull himself together. He told himself that at least he had seen some action before being captured. There were those who had fallen into enemy hands without having raised a weapon. Some of them had left everything behind in the United States in order to come to fight for the Fatherland, but the furthest they had got was a British internment camp. And at least he had not been injured. There were plenty of men who lay in prison camps in Britain nursing serious wounds. So he was, in a way, one of the fortunate ones. But that line of thought just made him all the more restless. He was itching to get back into the fight and his mood was not improved by the announcement, on 23 May, that Italy, a former member with Germany and Austria-Hungary of the old Triple Alliance, had joined the war on the side of the Allies. 'Italy's mean betrayal hit us particularly hard', he wrote later.

Gunther Plüschow had been at Donington for about a month when there was an incident that proved diverting enough to lift the men's spirits, for a short time at least. It also gave Plüschow an idea.

It was a common sight for a large herd of wild deer to gather just on the other side of the barbed wire and, one evening towards the end of June, a small fawn had lost its mother and was running back and forth alongside the fence. The prisoners began to call it towards them and, surprisingly, the animal obliged, wriggling under the wire and into the camp, albeit perhaps with some help. After it had been duly petted, the fawn was picked up by a lieutenant and carried into the batmen's room, where it was intended it would be raised. It was a plan that did not get very far. Lieutenant Colonel Picot's deputy was the lieutenant who had driven into one of his own soldiers outside Castle Donington railway station on the day that Plüschow and his colleagues had arrived. He was a deeply unpopular individual – the sergeants went out of their way to stress to the prisoners that not every British officer behaved in this way and Plüschow felt that even the commandant viewed his deputy with contempt.

Somehow, the lieutenant heard about the fawn and sent for the German commanding officer.

'Is it true that there is an animal in the camp?' he wanted to know.

128

'Yes,' said the German, 'a fawn.'

'And it came through the wire?'

'Yes, it just crept through.'

The British lieutenant almost choked. If there was a hole in his fence large enough for an animal as big as a fawn to get through, then it must have been made by German prisoners trying to escape, he argued. He demanded to see the site of this apparent security breach at once. Oh, and the animal could not stay. It must be removed immediately.

What followed was a scene of pure farce. The guard was turned out and twenty soldiers with bayonets fixed surrounded the German lieutenant who had brought the fawn into the inner camp, and he and the innocent animal were escorted smartly to the inner gate which was opened with great ceremony. Then the outer gate was unlocked and the prisoner liberated the fawn that skipped away into the park. The whole process was then reversed.

It was a nonsense that amused the prisoners – and probably embarrassed the rank-and-file British soldiers – but there was also a serious side to the affair and, for the whole of the next day, the entire arrangement of fences and entanglements was carefully examined. Gunther Plüschow watched it all with a mixture of amusement and calculation. If the fawn could get into the camp, then the British lieutenant was correct when he said that it pointed to a flaw in Donington Hall's defences. So now, instead of lying on the grass staring aimlessly into the sky, dreaming of home, Plüschow began to stroll around the camp perimeter. Only when he found what he thought might be a weak spot, did he lie down and pretend to doze. And through half-closed eyes he mentally noted every coming and going of every sentry, his regular route and his habits.

Eventually, he settled on a spot where he thought it would be possible to scale the ring of fences and escape quickly into the cover of the surrounding parkland. There was only one problem: Plüschow had no real idea of where Donington Hall was. He could probably find his way back to Castle Donington itself. And he knew that the town was in the north of England; at least he knew from the length of the train journey that it was quite a long way north of his previous camp, which was near London. But he had neither map nor compass.

Then he remembered that, on the day of his arrival, a fellow German officer had said that he had been driven to Donington Hall from Derby and that, as the car had turned into Castle Donington, it had passed a long bridge. Plüschow thought that this town of Derby might be north of the camp, but he was not sure how far and, in that regard, the officer had been vague. Twenty-five miles perhaps? Fifty? Maybe even as many as eighty? Plüschow needed to find out and his chance came sooner than he had dared hope.

Such was the relaxed nature of life at Donington Hall camp that the guards and their charges often mixed freely. Plüschow had made friends with an older guard – many prisoner of war camp guards were old soldiers from home-service battalions – whom he liked and to whom he occasionally gave a few cigars (Plüschow himself was a non-smoker but tobacco was always a good currency to carry). He took to inviting the soldier for a glass of beer in the canteen and, after a few meetings, asked him whether he found camp life as tedious as did the prisoners. Surely, he could sometimes get out for a change of scenery?

The soldier said that, yes, now and again he managed to leave Donington Hall and cycle to Derby, where he went to the pictures (probably to the Midland Electric Theatre, a purpose-built cinema which had opened its doors for the first time five years earlier; it stood close to the road that led out of town to Castle Donington).

Plüschow seized his chance: 'Derby? Surely that's too far for an old soldier like you to cycle?'

The soldier was indignant: 'Too old? You don't know an English Tommy if you say that. I'll race anyone. I can be in Derby in three to four hours.'

In fact, as Plüschow would later be pleased to discover, Derby was less than ten miles away, a distance that the old sweat should

130

have been able to cycle comfortably in about an hour and which might be walked in about three or four. For now, though, the German decided that he had learned enough for one day. A week later, he quizzed his new friend once more.

Again pressing a few cigars into the soldier's hand, the German asked him to settle a bet: 'I've been having an argument with a brother officer. I think that this town of Derby lies to the north of here, but he is convinced that it is to the south. If you can help me win the bet, there'll be a jug of beer waiting for you in the canteen.'

Without pausing to consider whether he might be giving away too much information to an enemy, the soldier was happy to confirm that Derby was indeed to the north. Then he went off to claim his beer, leaving Plüschow to ponder his next move. He now knew how far away Derby lay, and in what direction. And he had identified a potential escape route from the camp itself. Now he needed an accomplice, someone who knew England better than he did, and who spoke English fluently. Such a man, Plüschow determined, was Oberleutnant Oskar T Trefftz of the Imperial German Navy.

Trefftz needed no encouragement to join the escape attempt and the pair set a date: Sunday, 4 July 1915.

131

Chapter 15

Breakout

Just nine weeks after he had first set foot inside Donington Hall, Gunther Plüschow prepared to take his leave of the rambling Gothic mansion. He and Oskar Trefftz had rehearsed aspects of their escape plan and on that Sunday morning both reported sick. At the 10am roll call their names were entered on the sick list and when the orderly sergeant inspected their respective rooms, he found them each of them in bed. Just after 4pm both men got up and dressed. Plüschow donned a blue sailor's jersey given to him by a naval prisoner, and then put on the dark blue suit that he had bought in Shanghai and which had seen him through his subsequent adventures. He stuffed an old cap into the pocket of his raincoat, which he made into a bundle, and into his suit pockets he placed his razor, a knife, a small mirror, a length of string and two pieces of rag that would serve as handkerchiefs. He counted out his money – he had the sum of £6 that he had either saved or borrowed, although goodness knew when he would be able to repay it – and then he was ready.

Neither man had any papers, forged nor otherwise, which was a major problem because, that very month, identity cards had been introduced in Britain. They also had precious little food to take with them, so Plüschow sustained himself by eating several buttered rolls. Then he sought out his old friend, Siebel, whom he would dearly have loved to accompany him, but Siebel spoke hardly any English and, in any case, Plüschow thought his best chance of escape would be in the company of a sailor, not a fellow airman.

By now it was raining heavily as one of those fierce storms that erupt to throw a dark blanket over the brightest summer's day raged over this corner of Middle England, but after bidding farewell to their brother officers, Plüschow and Trefftz, together with Siebel, went outside. If the sentries wondered why three German prisoners had suddenly decided to take a walk in the park on such an awful afternoon, they were not in the mood to enquire. The sky was leaden, the rain sheeted down and the guards just plodded up and down in front of their sentry boxes. Wet and miserable, they dreamt of the end of their duty, the warmth of their billets and mugs of steaming tea. Mad German officers wandering about in the pouring rain was not a concern.

The trio made for the park's thatched summerhouse which was surrounded by shrubs but which afforded a good view right up to the fences. Once inside, Plüschow and Trefftz sat down by a wall and Siebel propped some garden chairs around them. Then, without another word, he left, making his way back to the hall by a different route so that no sentry would have seen three men go out, but only one of them return.

All Plüschow and Trefftz could now do was wait for the next stage of their plan. They did not speak to each other. Indeed, they hardly dared breathe. The minutes ticked away agonizingly slowly, the rain still hammered on the summerhouse roof, and the skies grew ever darker despite the fact that it was still only late afternoon in the middle of an English summer. Yet the appalling weather was proving an ally. It prevented off-duty British soldiers from wandering about the park, as they would have done on a fine summer's evening. And that left Plüschow and Trefftz in splendid isolation in the summerhouse.

Eventually the two men heard a clock strike six. Then they heard the bell ringing for roll call. Plüschow could also hear his heart thumping against his chest. The next few minutes would determine the immediate success, or failure, of their venture.

Half an hour elapsed and there was nothing but silence. Plüschow and Trefftz dared to relax for a moment; the first part of their plan appeared to have succeeded. During roll call, both men had again been reported as sick. For days, Plüschow had watched the orderly officer take the same route as he made his inspection: Trefftz's room first, then Plüschow's. Now a man from Plüschow's room took Trefftz's place in bed and, once that room had been checked, two men ran to Plüschow's room. When the officer arrived there, he found that each bed was occupied. And, with everything seemingly in order, the night boundary was closed. Plüschow and Trefftz settled down again. They still dared not speak to each other, but they exchanged smiles and supportive glances. At 10.30pm came the second test. First they heard the order to 'Stand to', and then, from an open window, the singing of 'Die Wacht am Rhein'. It signalled that the second hurdle was about to be negotiated. Again, the duty officer saw that all the beds were occupied. At 11pm a loud cheer rang out. It was the signal to the escapees that they would not now be missed until at least the morning.

By now the rain had stopped but still Plüschow and Trefftz dared not emerge from their hiding place. At midnight the guard would be changed and, only after that, were things likely to settle down. The sentries continued to pace back and forth, every fifteen minutes calling out to each other. Eventually the orderly officer arrived with the new guard and, once it had taken over, he shone his lamp over the day boundary for the last time and the old guard gratefully squelched their way back to their billets.

Some thirty minutes into 5 July 1915, Gunther Plüschow and Oskar Trefftz got up, stretched their aching legs, and slowly edged their way around the pile of chairs that Fritz Siebel had placed around them. They felt their way to the door of the summerhouse and peered out. Rainwater dripped from the guttering and from the trees and bushes. In the distance they saw the lights from the arc lamps that illuminated the night boundary, beyond which lay their freedom. Leaving Trefftz by the door, Plüschow crawled towards the spot he had selected for their escape. Eventually he reached the wire, confirmed it was the right place and that there were no sentries about, and then crawled back to where Trefftz was waiting. Then both men returned to the wire by the same route.

The first barbed wire fence was 9ft high and, about every 8ins, the wire was covered with long spikes. Plüschow and Trefftz wore leather leggings to protect them from the spikes, and they had also wound puttees around their knees and donned leather gloves. None of this, though, would be much use against another wire, 30ins from the ground, which was connected to the electricity supply. If either of the men touched that, it would trigger an alarm that would bring sentries running from every direction.

Each man carried a small bundle. Plüschow handed his to Trefftz and climbed over the fence, the makeshift protective clothing proving little help against the barbs and spikes. Then Trefftz threw over the two bundles and also scaled the fence. Both men were already badly scratched. And they still had two more obstacles to negotiate. The first was an arrangement of wire that stood about 3ft high and was about 30ft wide. They just ran at it, and through it, eventually arriving on the other side, torn and bleeding. Then there was the final fence, exactly similar to the first, complete with electrified alarm wire. Again they managed it but not without further injury – and Plüschow also lost the seat of his trousers which he managed to retrieve for later repair.

Now it only remained for them to sneak past the guardhouse on the road that ran past the camp, and then Donington Hall would be behind them. Even that was not an easy journey. In pitch darkness they had to cross a stream, climb a wall and scramble through a deep ditch before they reached the entrance to the park. But then, suddenly, they were on the open road. For a good twenty minutes they ran down that road, towards Castle Donington. In the small hours of the morning, in the summer of 1915, it was deserted and eventually they stopped to take stock of their situation. Off came their leggings and gloves – when they inspected their hands and legs they found them covered in deep scratches – and then they opened their bundles and put on their civilian grey raincoats before setting off again.

As they approached Castle Donington, they were aware that it would now be much more likely that they would meet someone. So they began their plan of action, walking briskly and cheerfully as if they were two old pals coming home after a particularly good night out. They were on the outskirts of the town when they saw a figure in the distance, striding towards them. They stopped and, in the darkness, Trefftz pulled Plüschow towards him. The pair embraced and a British soldier viewed the 'courting couple' with some interest as he passed them by. As they watched him disappear up the road, Plüschow could have sworn that it was none other than the sergeant-major from Donington Hall camp.

On their way again, Plüschow and Trefftz had no further scares as they walked through the main street of Castle Donington and on towards the bridge that they had been told stood on the junction of the road to Derby. The problem was that, from here, there was not one, nor even two choices of road to take, but three. The night was still pitch-black for, although the rain had stopped, thick cloud obscured the moon and stars and there was, of course, nothing in the way of street lighting. In the twenty-first century it is difficult to imagine how black as ink was the British countryside at night over ninety years ago. On that night, however, the problem was solved when Trefftz bumped into a cast-iron signpost. In the Second World War, nearly all signposts in Britain would be removed for fear of helping an invader but in 1915 it was still possible to be guided by them. As were Plüschow and Trefftz after Trefftz had shinned up this one, felt around and made out the word 'Derby' in raised letters. Now confident, they set off for their first objective.

The plan was to walk to Derby where they would catch a train to London and then stow away on a neutral merchant ship bound for the continent. It should then be a relatively easy task to get to Germany. After about an hour, the clouds began to part and the Pole Star appeared to aid their navigation. The road became a little busier, with the occasional motor vehicle speeding past them. They also began to meet more pedestrians but none seemed to take much notice of them. They ate some of the ham and chocolate they had brought with them, but they had nothing to drink and were now very thirsty. At first they licked rainwater from leaves and then tried their luck with a small pool but the water was rank. Thanks to their exertions, and their nervousness, they had both sweated profusely and their clothes were uncomfortably sticky.

Around dawn, which was heralded by a superb crimson sunrise that lifted their hearts, they reached the village of Alvaston on the outskirts of Derby. Here they crept into a garden where they shaved, rather painfully with the aid of a Gillette razor and saliva, and where Plüschow repaired his trousers. Then they each put on a collar and tie, dumped everything for which they had no further use, and went on their way, walking into the town on that Monday morning down London Road. In 1915, Derby boasted three railway stations and, as luck would have it, the one that served London – the Midland station – was just off London Road. Plüschow and Trefftz turned into Midland Road and strolled past the premises of W W Winter, the town's leading photographer who was a regular visitor to Donington Hall to take specially commissioned pictures of its officer-class prisoners.

At the station, the pair parted, resolving to meet up again on the steps of St Paul's Cathedral later that day. Plüschow bought a third-class ticket to Leicester, about half an hour's train ride away, where he alighted, purchased a ticket to London and then reboarded the train. He found Trefftz in the same compartment but the two ignored each other. Around noon, the train pulled into St Pancras and, after a heart-fluttering moment when the ticket collector at the barrier appeared to look at him more intently than he thought was normal, Gunther Plüschow walked out into Euston Road and was swallowed up in the crowd thronging wartime London.

Chapter 16

A Flame of Righteous Anger

By July 1915, Londoners had experienced the horrors of war first hand. The previous December, Britons had seen enemy action on the home front for the first time when the Kaiser's warships had shelled Hartlepool, Whitby and Scarborough. The first air raids had come on 19 January 1915 when two Zeppelin naval airships bombed Great Yarmouth, and Martha Taylor, aged 72, and Samuel Smith, a 53-year-old shoesmith, became Britain's first-ever air-raid victims. And only five weeks before Gunther Plüschow stepped off a train at St Pancras, the war had come much closer to London itself. On 31 May 1915, a Zeppelin dropped explosive and incendiary bombs on the docks area around the East End. Before the year was out, there would be Zeppelin raids on central London too. Londoners were being killed, property destroyed and, in the absence of a visible enemy, anger was turned towards German immigrants who had lived in London for years. This was certainly not a good time for a German airman to be wandering around the capital.

In fact, Plüschow was fortunate in that the time he had spent there two years earlier now stood him in good stead for getting around without much need to converse with the locals. First, though, he was ravenous and decided to spend some of his British money on a good meal; or four modest meals to be precise. To avoid drawing attention to himself, he visited four different restaurants where he ate medium-sized servings. Then, suitably refreshed, he decided to walk down by the Thames, trying to recall the landing stages in the Pool of London that he had last visited in 1913. If he and Trefftz were to sneak aboard a boat, then it would, as likely as not, have to be in this area.

But to his disappointment – and this was something that he had somehow not reckoned on – every landing stage was now heavily guarded, while vessels sailing under neutral flags were moored out in the middle of the river. Of course, this was wartime. His attempts to find a newspaper that gave shipping schedules also failed, probably for much the same reason.

Plüschow had another, much greater, disappointment awaiting him. His rendezvous with Oskar Trefftz on the steps of St Paul's Cathedral had been scheduled for 7pm and he made his way up there from the river. But when various clocks struck seven, Trefftz did not appear. Plüschow waited. He waited until 9pm. And then he decided to give up. His friend had probably already managed to stow away and was, even now, on his way across the Channel. If that was so, then good luck to him, thought Plüschow. But now he had to find somewhere to spend the night. He could not book into a hotel because hotel proprietors had to insist on guests producing their identity cards or passports.

He was hungry again and decided to get something to eat in a pub while he considered what to do next. The establishment he chose was a gloomy place and a glass of warm stout and a lump of cake was all it had to offer. Plüschow sat there until closing time which, thanks to recently imposed new licensing hours, was about 9.30pm in London. He and Trefftz had been on the run for the best part of a day and he wondered at what point their absence from Donington Hall had been discovered, and what sort of a hue and cry had followed. A few weeks later, Captain Franz von Rintelen, who had been working under cover in the neutral United States before being arrested on his way back to Germany, arrived at Donington Hall. He wrote later: 'To my astonishment I was cut by all the German officers there. At first I did not know why, but I gathered later that they took me for an English spy. Gunther Plüschow, the aviator from Tsingtao, had recently escaped, and they thought I was stationed there to find out how he had got away.'

Back on the streets of London, Plüschow wondered again where he would spend the night. He walked west, away from the little streets around the river. Eventually, small houses, shops and workplaces gave way to palatial mansions. By now, Plüschow could hardly put one foot in front of the other. Apart from a few hours spent on the train, he had been on his feet for the best part of twenty-four hours. He had to find somewhere to lie down and with one last effort he jumped over a low fence and into a garden where he curled up behind a thick box hedge. His resting place was barely a foot from the pavement, but now he hardly cared.

After about an hour, the French windows of the house in whose garden he had found himself opened and a small party of men and women spilled on to the verandah. The men wore evening suits, the women looked so elegant in their long evening dresses and they all seemed so happy, chattering away on this summer's evening. Then Plüschow heard music – a piano, and a beautiful soprano voice – and suddenly he was being entertained by a selection of melodies by Schubert. It seemed almost surreal. Finally, exhaustion overcame him and he slipped into a fitful sleep, lulled by the songs of Franz Peter.

It was the rays of the early sun that awakened him on that Tuesday morning, bathing his tired body in welcoming warmth. On the pavement, not far from his head, he heard the measured tread of a policeman strolling up and down the street. Plüschow wondered why the officer was patrolling this particular area and it worried him. Then he had his answer: a door opened and a pretty housemaid appeared. The policeman was at her side in an instant and the two were soon deep in conversation. Plüschow took his chance and, with one hand on the garden fence, vaulted back into the street and was away. He looked at his wristwatch: it was 6am. He walked on and eventually came to Hyde Park where he wandered across to a bench and stretched out. He doubted he would be noticed here. Other 'down and outs' were still slumbering peacefully nearby and Plüschow joined them, pulling his hat over his face and falling into a deep sleep.

When he woke again and looked at his watch once more, it was 9am. He stood up, stretched, and felt better. When he had entered Hyde Park, he had noticed an Underground station and he now made for this. Plüschow wanted to get back down to the river and he studied the Tube map and then bought a ticket back to the area. He wandered around again, wondering what had happened to Oskar Trefftz. That afternoon, he made his way into the Strand where he had his answer. According to Gunther Plüschow's later account, up and down the thoroughfare, large newspaper placards proclaimed: 'Hunt For Escaped German.' In fact, that day's newspapers did not trumpet the news, at least not in the papers themselves. The *Daily Sketch*, for instance, carried only the briefest report, buried away in the middle of the paper, almost lost among the rest of the war news. The one-column item read:

ESCAPES FROM DONINGTON HALL

ONE GERMAN OFFICER CAUGHT AT MILLWALL DOCKS; THE OTHER AT LARGE

Two prisoners of war escaped from Donington Hall yesterday morning and one of them, named Treppitz [*sic*] was captured last evening at Millwall Docks.

The other, Gunther Plüschow by name, is still at large. His description is: Height about 5ft 7ins, well-built, blue eyes, fair hair, fresh complexion, clean-shaven. He speaks English fairly well. So far as is known, he is wearing mufti.

Plüschow composed himself, bought a newspaper, went into a small café and began to devour the details. Trefftz must have made his way straight to the docks after they got off the train at St Pancras. In fact, Plüschow's erstwhile companion was already on his way back, not to Donington Hall but to Holyport, where many failed escapees were sent. Trefftz would later write to the authorities to complain about his treatment upon recapture.

Plüschow, meanwhile, had to act if his escape was not to be similarly doomed. One newspaper report had described him as 'smart and dapper', and although he already felt far from that, he now determined to remove any last doubts. From the Strand, he walked down Fleet Street and then towards the river again until he came to Blackfriars station, where he decided to leave his raincoat in the cloakroom. According to Plüschow, as he handed the coat over, the attendant asked him: 'What name is it?' Before he could think, Plüschow had replied: 'Meinen?' At which the attendant scribbled out a receipt and handed it to the German, who now saw that he was 'Mr Mine'. Thankful that his slip had resulted in nothing more than a new identity – something for which he had been searching, albeit a receipt from a station cloakroom was not so convincing as a passport – he nodded his thanks and turned away, trying not to seem in too much of a hurry.

From Blackfriars station, Plüschow walked along the banks of the Thames until he came to London Bridge. On the bridge he paused, looking downriver towards Tower Bridge. Beyond that famous landmark, steamers unloaded their cargoes, tugs snorted back and forth, and Thames barges cut through the water traffic. And down there somewhere, way off into the distance, on the Isle of Dogs, Oskar Trefftz's own bid for freedom had ended. Plüschow undid his collar and tie and dropped them into the river. Over the next hour or so, a mixture of coal dust, bootblack and Vaseline turned his fair hair black and greasy before a few minutes scrabbling about in a coal heap completed his transformation from Gunther Plüschow, escaped German naval flying officer, to George Mine, dock labourer, bargee, ship hand – he could take his pick. But wandering around London was not central to his plan, which was to board a vessel bound for a neutral port.

As Plüschow had already realized, this was not going to be an easy task and he could do little except wander about the capital – he never wanted to be far from the water – and wait for an opportunity to present itself. In the meantime, he could continue to read about himself as the newspapers published updates on his escape. He read that he had a high-pitched voice, had very good teeth 'which he shows prominently when smiling or talking', was very 'English in manner', knew England and Japan well, was 'quick and alert, both mentally and physically', and spoke both

English and French fluently. And, in due course, everyone would know that the escaped prisoner of war had an unusual distinguishing mark.

The *Daily Mail* was just one newspaper to report: 'Gunther Plüschow, the German naval lieutenant fugitive from Donington Hall, has been at large seven days. The Chinese dragon tattooed on his left arm while serving in the East should, however, betray his identity.'

That tattoo, of course, was well hidden under the blue naval sweater and the now well-worn suit jacket, which he left undone in the manner he imagined a member of the low working class would adopt. When he was walking through the streets, he stuffed his hands in his trouser pockets and, as he recalled later, he whistled and spat a lot. At night, he caught a few hours fitful sleep wherever he could.

Plüschow was already beginning to discount the possibility of stowing away on a boat in the London docks, but on his third day in the capital – on the morning of Wednesday, 7 July – he enjoyed a stroke of luck. He had decided to take a ride on a bus and was sitting on the top deck in front of two businessmen. They were carrying on quite a conversation and Plüschow sat transfixed as they spoke about a Dutch ship that dropped anchor at Tilbury every afternoon and which sailed for the port of Flushing at 7am every day. He left the bus at the next stop, went back to Blackfriars station and, an hour later, he was in Essex, standing on the dockside at Tilbury.

On the north bank of the Thames sea reach, Tilbury Docks – three parallel branch docks linked to one main dock, with transit sheds and a hotel – had opened for business in 1886 when steam vessels were taking over the shipping trade and access to deeper water became more important than being close to the City. A major feature was Tilbury Fort, originally built to defend London from attack from the sea, much added to over the centuries, but the one military success of its 350-year existence, when anti-aircraft guns on its parade ground shot down a Zeppelin, still a year away.

Plüschow arrived there around midday as dock workers made for the surrounding public houses that were taking advantage of the couple of hours' lunchtime opening they were allowed under wartime regulations. He looked around for the Dutch steamer but, of course, it had not yet arrived so he decided to get something to eat. Inside the establishment he selected, about 100 workmen were seated at long tables, shovelling huge plates of food into their mouths. Plüschow paid over 8d and in return received a plate piled high with potatoes, vegetables and large chunks of meat. A pint of ale from the bar completed the feast and he sat down, trying to look as inconspicuous as possible. He later wrote that, in trying to copy the table manners of his fellow diners, he almost came to grief when attempting to balance peas on his knife. Whether he made that comment in order to point out that these were low-bred fellows and he was uncomfortable in such company is open to conjecture. Whatever, in the middle of his meal he suddenly felt a tap on his shoulder. It sent a shiver down his spine. Was the game up?

Well, almost. It was a man whom Plüschow assumed was the proprietor, asking to see his identity papers. Of course, Plüschow could only say that he had left them behind, whereupon the man motioned Plüschow to follow him. Telling the German to wait, the he went into another room. It had a glass panel in the door and Plüschow watched as the man picked up a telephone and made a call, all the while looking back at this guest with no papers, who in turn was eyeing the door to the street, wondering what were the chances that he could run out and disappear into the street.

Before Plüschow had decided on the best course of action, the man returned: 'If you haven't any papers, then I can't help you. Anyway, what's your name? Where are you from?'

'George Mine,' Plüschow told him. 'I'm an American from the *Ohio*. It's a four-masted barque just upstream. I just came in for something to eat. I've paid for my dinner. I just haven't got my papers with me.'

'Well,' said the man, 'this is a private club. Only members are

145

allowed in. You should know that. But if you join, then you can come in and eat as often as you like.'

It was an offer that Plüschow thought it best to accept. He paid over the 3s membership fee, then tied the resultant piece of red ribbon through the buttonhole of his suit jacket, to signify that he was now a fully paid-up member of a dockside workingmen's club. That done, he wandered back to his table, as nonchalantly as his pounding heart would allow, and took a long drink of his stout. He picked over his food, though. Suddenly, his appetite had quite disappeared.

Plüschow now had to locate the Dutch steamer. He wandered down to the river again and lay down on the bank, pretending to doze but in reality keeping his eyes fixed firmly on the incoming shipping. Eventually, at about 4pm his heart began to race again. Coming upriver was a fast steamer flying the Dutch flag. By the time it had drawn level with Plüschow it had slowed right down, dropping anchor and tying up to a buoy right in front of him. His spirits rose, especially when he saw the steamer's name: *Mecklenburg*. Wasn't his own family from Mecklenburg-Schwerin? This had to be a good omen? Perhaps, although the 2,885-ton SS *Mecklenburg* of the Stoomvaart Mij. Zeeland company was a doomed ship; seven months later it would be sunk after being mined while travelling from Tilbury to Flushing.

Plüschow's plan was a simple one. He caught a ferry and crossed the river to Gravesend from where he would, that night, take a barge out to the buoy, climb the hawser, stow away on the *Mecklenburg* and, with any degree of good fortune, this time tomorrow he would be on his way to Holland. In the meantime, he had to find somewhere to wait and, after making sure that he was not being observed, he climbed over a pile of wood and rubbish, then crawled under some planks where he was pleas-antly surprised to find several bundles of hay. It wasn't Berlin's Hotel Kaiserhof. It wasn't even the spartan quarters offered by Donington Hall. But it did provide a warm billet while he waited for nightfall.

Around midnight, when everything around him had quietened

down, Plüschow climbed out of the nest he had made for himself. It was raining heavily and he had difficulty in negotiating the planks and rubbish. His endeavours were not helped by the fact that it was now pitch-black and he struggled to locate either of the barges he had noted that afternoon. Eventually, he found them, but the tide was out and the barges were now high and dry on the foreshore; there was no way that he could drag one into the water. Then he spotted a small dinghy bobbing about on the water's edge. That would do. But as he moved forward towards the plank that led across the foreshore to the dinghy, Plüschow suddenly found the ground slipping from under his feet. Before he knew it, he was knee-deep in an evil-smelling bog, and sinking still deeper. He managed to get his left hand on to the plank and then, with a superhuman effort, haul himself back on to firmer ground. He was too exhausted to try again. Instead, he picked his way back to his den, where he lay until sunrise.

Local Thames watermen were already servicing ships in Gravesend Reach when, just after 7am, Gunther Plüschow sat on a bench in the park that overlooked the water there and watched the SS *Mecklenburg* slip anchor and make for the open sea without him. Then he stood up and wearily made his way back to London, wandering around almost in a daze at times, at others studying the dozens of neutral ships loading and unloading, and hoping for that single moment when he might slip aboard one unnoticed. But no such opportunity presented itself and, after eating in a slum of an East End café, Plüschow decided to return to Gravesend.

It was well into the evening by the time he arrived and, as he was making his way to his previous night's accommodation, he saw a new steamer moored in the river. The SS *Prinses Juliana* was a sister ship to the *Mecklenburg*. Also owned by the SMZ company, and of similar tonnage to the *Mecklenburg*, she too could carry more than 300 passengers on her regular route between Tilbury and the Netherlands. As it turned out, she would meet a similar fate – and before the *Mecklenburg* met hers. On 1 February 1916, on her way from Flushing to Tilbury, the

Prinses Juliana would strike a mine off Felixstowe. Grounded there, she would break in two parts during a gale on the night of 29 March the same year. In fact, during the First World War, the neutral Dutch would be hit hard by the U-boat offensive of mine-laying and torpedoing, to the point where the Netherlands government laid up several of its largest and most valuable liners for the duration. For now, though, the *Prinses Juliana* was in one piece and Plüschow resolved to try to board her that night. This time, however, he would find a better spot from which to reach his target.

It was midnight and pouring with rain when he again left his den and made for the point he had selected, a stony part of the bank with no visible signs of the slimy morass that had dogged his original bid. Hiding his jacket and boots – hockey boots actually, given to him by his captors – under a stone, he pushed his stockings, watch, razor and mirror into his cap and jammed that on his head. Then he walked into the water – the tide was going out – and began to swim towards a rowing boat that was anchored just offshore. But the water was bitingly cold, he was achingly tired and the weight of his clothes began to drag him down. The current grew faster and Plüschow's strength deserted him. The next thing he knew, he was lying on some flat stones. Only the fact that the river bent sharply had washed him ashore and saved him from being swept out to sea by the fast-flowing current. Plüschow dragged himself to his feet and stumbled back to where he had hidden his jacket and boots. Putting them back on – and what an effort even that proved – he managed to get back to his hiding place. He was trembling and his teeth rattled together because of the cold. Sleep proved impossible so he got up and ran around for a while to try to keep warm. Then dawn arrived and, still wet and thoroughly dispirited, he went back to London to spend most of the day trying to dry off and warm up in several churches.

By mid-afternoon Plüschow felt as though some of his strength had returned and, after a meal in yet another of the East End's low dives, in the middle of a public square he came across a recruiting drive. The main speaker was making an impassioned plea for able-bodied males to join the King's colours – it would be January 1916 before the British government introduced the first of a series of Military Service Acts that set out conscription regulations – but not one man in the watching crowd moved towards the platform. So recruiting sergeants began to move among them.

Before he knew it, one of them was looking down on Plüschow. The soldier, who must have been well over 6ft tall, reached out and squeezed the German's forearms before trying to get him to enlist. Plüschow said that he couldn't as he was an American citizen but that did not put off the sergeant who produced a card showing various British Army uniforms printed in bright colours. Eventually, Plüschow managed to take his leave by promising to speak with the captain of his ship. If the skipper agreed, then Plüschow would return the following day and join up.

Of course, the German never went near this part of London again. Indeed, the following day saw him visiting in the British Museum and a number of picture galleries as well as matinee performances at the music hall. Anything to relieve the boredom, keep warm and regain his strength. That evening he sat in the park at Gravesend and listened to a military band, all the time acutely aware that he now looked like an utter down and out. He had already noticed that people on buses were now giving him a wide berth, probably because it had been almost a week since he had been able to take a bath.

He had now abandoned his plan to swim to the *Prinses Juliana*, which lay there, tantalizingly close but still too far away, given the strong current in the Gravesend Reach. If he were to reach the steamer, it would have to be by another craft of some kind or other. There was one possibility: a dinghy lay moored against a wharf. The wharf seemed to be guarded day and night by a sentry, but there was no other option and just after midnight, his boots tied around his neck, Plüschow crept over the stone wharf in his stockinged feet and dropped the 6ft into the dinghy. The sentry was at the far end of his beat and when he returned, he crunched past the craft without a second glance at it.

Plüschow felt for the oars and, to his dismay, found that they were padlocked. But the chain was loose and he managed to free them. With the knife that he had carried between his teeth – by now he must have looked like the classic pirate – he cut the ropes that tied the dingy to the wharf, and then slowly eased the oars through the water towards the *Prinses Juliana*. But there was a further disaster awaiting him. When he had dropped into the boat, he had noticed that it had shipped some water. Now, as he rowed away from the wharf, the water rose rapidly and the boat began to sink. Moments later, however, there was a grinding sound and the dinghy bumped to a halt. The sudden change in the level of the river due to the tide had been remarkable. Plüschow looked in despair at his ludicrous situation: he was sitting in a boat that was brimful of water, but which was on a mound of stinking mud and going nowhere. He was high and dry, 15ft from the wall of the wharf, with the sentry marching up and down.

Taking stock of his situation, the bedraggled German quickly devised a plan. Removing his socks and rolling up his trouser legs as far as they would go, he picked up a boathook and, using it like a pole-vaulter, launched himself out of the dingy towards the wall. He was never going to reach the wharf in one leap, but he was still about 8ft short when he landed in what amounted to a quicksand of foul-smelling mud. He sank in it up to his knees before the relief of feeling a hard surface under his feet. Again, Plüschow summoned all his strength and managed to wade through the mud to the wall where he rested for a few minutes before securing the boathook to the top and somehow hauling himself 6ft back on to the wharf. He tottered towards the grass and collapsed, breathing heavily. Amazingly, the sentry had heard none of this commotion and carried on patrolling the wharf edge oblivious to the drama that had just been played out.

Plüschow again reviewed his situation. He was still as far away from the *Prinses Juliana*, and the capricious nature of the Thames had dogged his every attempt to reach her. And now he was in an even worse state than before: his legs were caked in cloying grey mud and there was no fresh water at hand to wash them even half clean. His only option was to wait until it dried and then scrape off as much as he could. Yet Gunther Plüschow wasn't going to give up. In fact, he was about to try again. Around 2am, the mud had dried sufficiently for him to be able to put his socks and boots on again. Then he wandered drunkenly towards the small bridge that was part of the sentry's patrol. He staggered right up to the soldier, who passed some comment about too much whisky, and then Plüschow was past him and lurching off into the distance.

After about 100yds he looked back and the sentry had disappeared, so Plüschow resumed a more sober gait until he reached the spot from where he had set off on the previous night's ill-fated swim. About 200yds from the shore he could make out a line of rowing boats and, again leaving his jacket and boots under some stones, he dropped back in the river. At first it seemed that this would be an easier swim that last time, but as he left the protection of the river bend, he was again swept up in the strong current. Somehow he kept going, eventually reaching the boats and hauling himself into the first one. But there was nothing with which to propel it – no oars, no boathook, nothing. Plüschow slid back into the water and tried another boat with similar result. In fact, all six were empty and he had no option but to swim back to the shore. Two hours after he had begun this latest ill-fated attempt, he was picking up his clothes from their hiding place. Thirty minutes after that he was falling into the hay in his now all-too-familiar night abode.

It seems quite remarkable, considering all that he had been through in the previous twenty-four hours, but Plüschow wrote later that the following morning he walked back 'up to London on foot' along the south bank of the Thames – a distance of over 20 miles. He would have been wearing wet clothes and his limbs must have been aching. And then, he wrote, he returned, also on foot, along the north bank to Tilbury. And not once, during that entire journey, did he come across even the slightest opportunity to slip unnoticed aboard one of the scores of ships, big and small, that he passed.

He was now at his lowest ebb since leaving Donington Hall. That evening he caught a train back to London and went to the music hall. He had £1 remaining of his escape money and he reasoned that he might as well spend some of it on a little enjoyment. Then he would try one last time to sneak aboard a neutral vessel in the docks. If that failed, as every other attempt had failed, then he would give himself up and follow in the footsteps of Oskar Trefftz. He might even see his old friend Fritz Siebel again.

Plüschow watched the performance from the topmost gallery – the cheap ticket in the so-called 'gods'. The name of the venue and the programme of entertainment are not recorded but he later wrote that when the *tableaux vivants* were unveiled, they were about the war and, naturally, portrayed Germany in defeat. He recalled the point at which Britannia appeared with a Palm of Victory in her left hand and a 'German soldier' in field grey prostrate beneath her right foot.

He wrote: 'I felt consumed by a flame of righteous anger, and in spite of the forcible protests of my neighbours, I fled the theatre and was able to catch the last train to Tilbury.'

According to Plüschow, the affront he felt at the portrayal of his country on a music-hall stage made him determined to succeed in his next bid for freedom. Back down at the Gravesend Reach, he spotted a scull moored near some fishermen's huts. It was late in the evening but there were people still about. However, their day's work done, the fishing folk were busy chatting, oblivious to all around them as a shabby figure walked through the gloom towards the shoreline and, not 20ft from where they sat, stepped gently into the tiny craft.

Cutting the scull free, Plüschow drifted silently towards a fishing boat, on the quarterdeck of which a woman was trying to get a baby to sleep. Still no one noticed him. The scull had no rowlocks – the swivelling device that holds an oar in place – and so Plüschow had to push off hard from the bank, out into the

Thames, and then paddle. Again the current seized him in its grasp, this time sweeping him towards a military pontoon bridge consisting of seventy Thames swim-head lighters – barges with flattened bows or sterns – that had been put into place at the start of the war to serve both as a barrier and as a rapid means of getting troops across the river between Gravesend and Tilbury. A sentry called out a challenge but the scull and its dishevelled occupant swept straight underneath the bridge and on downriver into the darkness.

Plüschow now had his work cut out, somehow trying to steer the little nutshell of a vessel on the racing ebb tide. He was still battling with the river when the scull came to juddering, albeit temporary, halt when it collided with the anchor cable of a coal tender. Before the scull was thrown free again, Plüschow managed to get a rope around the cable. Then, moored to the tender, he sat and waited as the outgoing Thames rushed past him for hour upon hour.

When dawn broke, the tide was still too strong for him to dare cast off again but eventually the river died down and he drifted downriver for about an hour until he came to an old bridge. The scull drifted towards the right-hand bank and Plüschow tied it up under the bridge on the south side of the Thames. He clambered up the bank and lay down in the long grass from where he watched the *Mecklenburg* steam past towards her home port.

Plüschow lay there for the next sixteen hours. Then he climbed back into the scull and let the incoming tide take him back upriver until he was again able to tie up to the same coal tender that had come to his rescue the previous night. The *Prinses Juliana* lay to starboard and, at about 1am, Plüschow pushed off from the tender and paddled towards the steamer. Heaving himself on to the *Prinses Juliana*'s buoy, he gave the scull one final kick, sending it downstream again, this time without its one-man crew. Finally, satisfied that his arrival had alerted no one, Plüschow began to climb the steel cable that connected the steamer to the buoy. He stuck his head over the rail, saw that the forecastle was empty, and hauled himself on to

153

the deserted deck. Then, slipping off his boots which he hid under a timber-pile, he began to investigate further in his stockinged feet. When he looked towards the cargo deck he saw two sentries apparently looking straight back at him. He stepped back and froze, but they had not seen him and, about half an hour later, he heard them engaged in conversation with female voices. Two stewardesses had apparently come off a late shift and the sentries were far more interested in them than in keeping a lookout for anything amiss. By now dawn was breaking and Plüschow knew that he must hide away completely. He climbed down on to the cargo deck, slipped past the sentries and their companions, and made for the promenade deck. There he climbed up a deck pillar to the seaward side of a lifeboat, managed to undo the tapes on the boat cover and hauled himself into the boat where he collapsed, the last dregs of his strength finally deserting him. Then he closed his eyes.

It was the ship's siren that awakened him as it heralded the steamer's arrival into the harbour at Flushing. After a week on the run, after suffering so many setbacks and disappointments, and after so many narrow squeaks, Gunther Plüschow had escaped from England. Whatever happened now, he was in the neutral Netherlands and no longer cared who knew his identity. He took out his knife and tore a large gash in the boat cover through which he climbed out on to the deck and waited to be arrested as a stowaway. But no one took any notice of him. The crew was far too busy making preparations to the tie up at the quayside, while passengers were simply concerned with locating their luggage and continuing their onward journey. It was only when he climbed the steps down to the promenade deck that he attracted any attention, and then mostly from women who seemed extraordinarily keen to give this dirty, unkempt figure as wide a berth as possible. Plüschow continued to the foredeck to reclaim his boots from under the pile of timber, put them on and then stood up, straightened his back and looked out across the wharves that lined the River Scheldt. He briefly considered making the acquaintance of the *Prinses Juliana*'s captain because

154

he did not wish any problems to befall the Stoomvaart Mij. Zeeland company for unknowingly having transported an escaped German prisoner of war. But common sense prevailed over good manners and he simply thrust his hands in his trouser pockets, trudged down the gangway, paused to give the crew a helping hand in fastening the ship to the quayside, and melted into the crowd of passengers.

There was one last hurdle to negotiate: everyone was having his or her papers checked. There was only one way out for Gunther Plüschow – through the door marked: 'Entry Forbidden'. He opened it and was free.

Chapter 17

Hero's Return

By the time that Gunther Plüschow arrived back in Schwerin towards the end of July 1915, the war in Europe had settled into a stalemate. British and French offensives on the Western Front had gained little ground. By the end of the year Germany would have suffered around another 612,000 casualties, the British a million, the French nearer two million. But the battle lines would be little changed. On the Eastern Front it was a different story. Germany and Austria-Hungary drove Russia from Lithuania and Poland. Bulgaria entered the war on Germany's side, encouraged by a promise of land at the expense of the Bulgarians' old enemy, Serbia.

For Plüschow, however, it was already unlikely that he would be returned directly to the front line, at least not in the West. He was already something of a legend and the 'Hero of Tsingtao' being recaptured by the British was something that the German High Command did not want to risk. They did, however, want to decorate him. Over the next few weeks, Plüschow received several awards including the Iron Cross, both First Class and Second Class, and the Royal House Order of Hohenzollern (a Prussian order bestowed upon officers only). The award that he was probably most attached to, however, was the Prussian version of the Imperial Pilot's Shield; surrounded by the familiar oak and laurel wreath, it showed a Taube in flight over a pastoral scene.

The hero, though, had not had an uneventful journey back to his hometown, even after successfully disembarking from the *Prinses Juliana* at Flushing. Two fellow countrymen had taken him under their wing in the Dutch port, although they also took some convincing that he was an officer who had escaped from

England. After a hot bath, his first for several weeks, and the best meal he had enjoyed during the same period, Plüschow had boarded a slow train to Germany. He had dressed in workmen's clothes and hoped to settle down unobtrusively for the journey. But before the train had even left the platform he felt a tap on his shoulder. It was a plain-clothed Dutch policeman.

'Secret service', he told Gunther, whose heart sank once more.

'Where have you come from?' he asked.

'England', Plüschow replied.

'Where are your papers?'

'I don't have any.'

'You came from England without papers? That couldn't have been easy.'

'It wasn't', Gunther agreed.

'Well,' said the man, 'I wish you a pleasant onward journey.'

They shook hands and Plüschow settled down, hardly daring to look up again until the train was well on its way. His mind was racing. One year earlier, as Europe had begun to smoulder then burst into flames, he had been on the other side of the world. Now, after the most incredible adventures, he was almost home. After about three hours of rumbling through the Dutch country-side the train slowed down once more as it neared another station. This time, however, Plüschow saw the black and white border post, on the other side of which lay Germany.

The train stopped at the little weaver city of Goch, just over the border, where two large men in field-grey uniforms took their duties more seriously than the Dutch secret service man, who perhaps had just wanted to send this strange character on his way out of the Netherlands. Plüschow tried to explain but the soldiers were not interested in his story. The following morning they took him the 19 miles to Wesel, the administrative centre for the district. His arrival there caused considerable interest among the locals because, Plüschow learned later, there were reports of a spy in the area. The prisoner was told to sit down and await a senior officer. When the man arrived, to Gunther's absolute delight it was someone he had known from his early days in the

Navy. After a good breakfast he was on a train to Berlin, this time carrying a temporary passport that would ease him on the remainder of his journey. There was a minor brush with an old general in full dress uniform who boarded the train at Münster and was outraged to see a first-class compartment being occupied by a man in working clothes. No amount of tidying up on Gunther's part would persuade the crusty old man to remain.

By the time the train rolled over the railway bridge that spanned the Elbe at Magdeburg, just over an hour from its final destination, Plüschow realized just how tired he was, as the tension of the last few months finally released him from its grip. At seven o'clock that evening, he stepped out of Berlin's Zoo station, to be greeted by his beloved Isot. His feeling of happiness as they walked into the street, hand in hand, was indescribable. The last twelve months suddenly seemed like a dream.

And so did the next few days as Plüschow went about buying new clothes – especially a new uniform. Promoted to lieutenant commander, over the next three years he was to command at least two important Imperial German Naval air stations: at Kiel-Holtenau where he hosted a visit by the Kaiserin, Princess Auguste Viktoria; and at Libau on the Baltic coast, where he and Isot were married in an aircraft hanger in June 1916. Their only son, Guntolf (he later took his father's first name) would be born two months before the Armistice that ended this most dreadful of wars.

In 1917, Gunther's account of his time in Tsingtao was published. *Die Abenteuer des Fliegers von Tsingtau* (The Adventures of the Airman of Tsingtau) quickly became a huge seller – by some accounts more than half a million copies were sold – and there was hardly a schoolboy in Germany who had not heard of the Hero of Tsingtao.

Plüschow was also in Flanders at some point later in the war. There is a suggestion that for a short time he was stationed at Zeebrugge. He certainly visited his elder brother, Hans, who was serving as a major in the Grand-Ducal Mecklenburg Fusilier Regiment Kaiser Wilhelm No. 90, part of the Schwerin-based

17th Division of the IX Army Corps that had fought with distinction throughout the war and had been engaged in almost every major battle on the Western Front. In July 1918, Gunther was given leave to bury his younger brother. Lieutenant Wolfgang Plüschow was killed in a flying accident at Euba in Saxony while attached to a flying school. Wolfgang was buried at Wismar, a small port on the Baltic coast, 18 miles north of Schwerin and birthplace of many of the Plüschow family.

As Wolfgang was laid to rest alongside his father and sister, Germany's fortunes began to wane dramatically. The Aisne–Marne offensive ended their series of victories that had begun on the Somme in March 1918. The way was now open for the great Allied offensive that would start at Amiens on 8 August that year. The German Army began to collapse. On 3 November, Austria signed a peace settlement with the Allies. On 11 November, Germany followed suit, the Kaiser having abdicated two days earlier.

In July, Plüschow had been posted to the air station at Seddin near Stolp in East Prussia from where, earlier in the war, naval airships had flown bombing and reconnaissance missions mostly over the Eastern Front. In its heyday, the Seddin station consisted of a landing site for dirigibles, two airship halls – one fixed double shed, one fixed small single shed – a hydrogen production facility, storage and workshops. It was here that Gunther's war ended.

Telegrams and letters charting the crisis had been coming across his desk for weeks but the communiqué telling him that the Kaiser had abdicated left him feeling empty, drained of almost all emotion. Military installations were instructed to take down all flags and emblems. So it had come to this. Plüschow looked down at his own uniform that suddenly seemed to represent nothing. He refused to allow the Imperial German flag to be taken down, barking at the soldier who was trying to do so. But then the stark realization swept over him and he relented, taking the flag home with him to the house in the woods where he and Isot and their baby son had made their home.

He remained in the military for a few months but after the Treaty of Versailles of June 1919, which required Germany and its allies to accept total responsibility for the war and made Germany in particular pay in the most swingeing terms, he began to reconsider his future. That month Rear Admiral Ludwig von Reuter, rather than let it be divided up by the Allies, ordered the scuttling of the Imperial High Seas Fleet as it lay in internment at the Royal Navy base at Scapa Flow in the Orkney Islands. Crew indiscipline had already been rife – in October 1918 there had been a major mutiny by sailors who had no intention of being sacrificed in the final weeks of a war that was clearly lost – and naval unrest had quickly spread. From November 1918 until the formal establishment of the Weimar Republic in August 1919, Germany was in a state of revolution. Gunther Plüschow was weary and sickened by it all. At the age of 33 he officially resigned from the Imperial German Navy. Now he needed a job.

Chapter 18

Restless Feet

By 1920 the vanquished empire of Kaiser Wilhelm II lay in ruins. The geography of Europe was being redrawn as Germany was made to suffer large territorial losses. In all it lost one million square miles of land – 28,000 of them in Europe – and six million subjects. The Treaty of Versailles that blamed Germany for the war dictated that reparations, eventually set at £6,600 million, would be paid in monthly instalments. In addition the Germans had to rebuild their economy but the loss of their colonies – Tsingtao had been one of their first overseas bases to be lost – and land ceded to other countries deprived them of rich sources of raw materials. The political impact in Germany itself was enormous. The government of the day refused to sign the Treaty and resigned. The incoming administration had no choice but to agree. And as the economy collapsed – and many old soldiers wondered how Germany could have lost the war when they had still held French territory taken at the very outset in 1914 – the argument that it was the politicians, not the military, who had been responsible for national humiliation gained huge support. It would not be long before millions of Germans distrusted the Weimar Republic in all its manifestations, with devastating consequences not only for Germany but also for the entire civilized world.

Whoever was to blame, Gunther Plüschow certainly hated the mess in which his country now found itself. Desperately worried about the prospect of a civil war, he joined one of the local citizen militias that had been formed to keep the peace and combat looters, but it was not called into action. Amid all this chaos he tried to get on with life. He had a wife and an infant son to support and he looked around for a job or a business opportunity, preferably one that involved flying. There were plenty of spare aircraft lying around and he was a flyer – and a good writer (his bestselling book *Die Abenteuer des Fliegers von Tsingtau* had by now been translated into several languages). He based himself in Berlin and approached several newspapers, offering his services as a 'flying journalist', delivering the news between Johannisthal and Weimar, to where the seat of government had been relocated after violence on the streets of the capital. Early in 1919 the Deutsche Luft Reederei company began flying mail, but especially newspapers. Later that year, when it began transporting passengers, it was the first scheduled air service in Europe and came to form part of what would become the first sustained airline service in the world.

Plüschow began to fly alongside the company that would, through several amalgamations, eventually become Lufthansa. The Deutsche Luft Reederei service used modified former military AEG and DFW biplanes; Germany, of course, was now forbidden to have an air force. One of Plüschow's fellow pilots was Arthur Neumann, who four years later would be part of Roald Amundsen's failed attempt to fly across the North Pole from Wainwright in Alaska to the Norwegian island of Spitsbergen.

By then, Gunther had tried a number of jobs as the German economy was wrecked by a hyperinflation that wiped out savings and took thousands of companies to the wall. By the second half of 1923, prices would rise fivefold every week. A measure of the problem can be seen in the cost of a simple postage stamp. In 1920, the highest valued stamp issued was 4 marks; three years later it was 50 billion marks. By 1924 hyperinflation would have radically redistributed the wealth of Germany. If the poor had little to lose in the first place, and if the very richest segment of society had managed to convert their wealth into forms untouched by the problem of rampant inflation, then the people that were hardest hit were the middle and upper-middle classes. Even in the early days of this financial crisis Plüschow's capital was dwindling, his income never certain, his mind racing as he thought about ways to make ends meet.

Night after night spent in lonely hotel rooms, as he waited to fly back to Isot and Guntolf, saw him drafting and redrafting his plans. He was able to take his military pension and that helped, but the thought of collecting a pension when he was still in his mid-30s still depressed him. Eventually he managed to move the family back to Berlin, but as inflation increased he was still having to ask Isot: 'Do we have enough for bread?' It was like swimming against a current even stronger than the one that had pushed him back on those dark nights down by the Thames.

Then, in the middle of a harsh winter, he lost his flying job. Never before in all his life had he been unemployed. It hit him hard and he took to sitting in the beer cellar, nursing a stein and trying to work out another plan. He was hardly the stereotype morose drinker; it was just a place where he could sit and reflect. One night a fellow drinker recognized Gunther and offered him a job as a cinema projectionist. That suited him – he was becoming interested in cinematic art – but the pay was poor. However, just as Plüschow's reputation had helped him land the cinema job, so it suddenly opened the door to a much better position as a car salesman at a showroom on the Kurfürstendamm, one of the most famous thoroughfares in Berlin.

Gunther soon became the star salesman, not least because he could call on his many contacts to shop there rather than elsewhere. But the banks had resorted to printing money and unfortunately they could not print it fast enough, so as good a salesman as he was, business was drying up and he could foresee problems ahead for his employer. There was also the continuing problem of unrest on the streets. One morning Gunther arrived to open up the showroom but decided against it when there was trouble outside. Instead he got a message to Isot: 'Buy some food and then stay indoors. Don't leave the house.'

Yet, as Isot admitted later, their life was probably better than most, relatively speaking at least. Her husband's main problem was that he was unsettled. He knew that he had to do anything to put food on the table, but it was the technical side of the motor trade that interested him, not selling cars but building and maintaining them. He began to talk about setting up his own business selling cars and motor cycles, although he could not help but reflect what it would be like for the hero of Tsingtao to become a car mechanic. It might seem odd that, when he could see all around him collapsing, Gunther would even consider such a venture. But he had an unshakable belief in his ability to survive, and his wife also had implicit trust in her husband to do the right thing.

So the business was duly started and, when it needed premises, Isot, supportive as ever, raided her jewelry box; four weeks later Gunther Plüschow was opening his own motor business in the centre of Berlin, complete with a shiny sign over the door.

It was now the winter of 1923 – another bitter winter at that – and Gunther, ever aware of the importance of publicity, had another plan. He built a motor cycle and entered it into a twenty-four-hour endurance race on the Automobil-Verkehrs-und Übungs-Strasse (AVUS) track that ran through the Grunewald forest on the south-western outskirts of Berlin. The track, which had been opened in 1921 after being started by Russian prisoners during the war, originally comprised two straights, each approximately 6 miles long, with a hairpin corner at each end. Racing there must have presented quite a spectacle. According to Isot, Gunther's machine won the race, claimed the world record for the event and took pride of place in his showroom window as a great advertisement for the new venture.

It was exciting, and initially rewarding, but still he mused – it was not the same as 'flying up in the clouds'. Eventually the business, like countless others, seems to have failed in those increasingly dire times, and once again Gunther's only guaranteed source of income was from giving lectures. The hero of Tsingtao was always in demand as a raconteur. It just did not pay very much.

It was back to the beer cellar in the hope of making new

contacts. Isot now joined her husband at these 'networking' sessions and soon Gunther was offered a position as a representative for a steelmaking firm. The job took him to Belgium, Italy and Spain, and when he was scheduled to go to England, he took Isot with him and was able to show her the haunts around London where he had waited to escape, and the Home Counties, where he had been imprisoned. On the journey he was even able to show her Flushing where he had stepped through the door marked 'Entry Forbidden' and freedom.

But travelling around Europe selling steel was not enough for the man of action who had flown alone against the Japanese, the man who had escaped Germany's enemies by travelling halfway around the world. As he gritted his teeth and got on with whatever boring job he could obtain, Isot watched his spirits sink lower and lower. And realizing that she could never really expect him to settle down to anything other than a life of adventure, she made a suggestion: many of his old comrades were now in the merchant marine; perhaps he should update his sailing qualifications so that he might also find work there.

Gunther took little persuading and after passing an examination as a boat captain he was offered a job with a company that took tourists cruising in the Mediterranean. On his first trip, the boat called at Gibraltar, yet another trip down a memory lane that he would probably rather have forgotten.

Several weeks later Isot received a letter from him, from Greece. Gunther had met an old acquaintance, Erich Ferdinand Laeisz, who had offered him a position on the *Parma*, leaving Hamburg for Tierra del Fuego that autumn. Plüschow's thoughts must have gone back to that day a quarter of a century earlier when he had sat in the Imperial Military Academy's library at Gross-Lichterfelde and gazed at pictures of mountain peaks, glaciers, waterfalls and forests in that so remote part of the world. He had accepted the chance and now wanted Isot to buy a still-photo camera and a cine camera. One of his jobs on board would be to record the voyage. At last he was off on another adventure.

On 15 September 1925, Gunther Plüschow set sail on the 3,091-ton steel four-masted barque *Parma* that had been built at Port Glasgow in 1902, one of four sailing ships of the Laeisz shipping line that carried nitrate from German mines in Chile to German factories on the Elbe. After calling at the Falkland Islands, the *Parma* rounded Cape Horn before sailing north up the coast of Chile where she docked at Valdivia, since the mid-nineteenth century the home of a sizeable German community who had been given land and settled in the surrounding areas and stamped their mark upon the city.

Plüschow left the *Parma* at Valdivia and, after accepting several invitations to lecture on his Tsingtao exploits to the German colony, he joined the coastal steamer *Apolo* and journeyed south again, to the province of Última Esperanza. It was an area that immediately captured Gunther's imagination with some of the most spectacular mountain peaks in South America, not to mention being the home of much of the Southern Patagonian Ice Field. It was also a region that had been little explored and together with Richard Lauezzari, a German national who managed a ranch for the Sociedad Explotadora de Tierra del Fuego, Pluschow spent several days riding through the area on horseback. It was a remarkable experience with guanacos (a smaller cousin to the alpaca and llama), rheas (large fast birds, like an ostrich) and condors just some of the local wildlife that took Gunther's breath away.

He was to write later:

> The view was out of our wildest dreams . . . Incredible wild countryside . . . in fading colours the High Cordilleras, the fantastic towers and pinnacles, enormous glaciers that glowed and shimmered like a heavenly Colossus.

One day they came to some impressive mountain peaks. The Torres del Paine ranged from 7,415ft to 8,204ft, which may not sound too daunting to an experienced climber but which could be lashed by 100mph snowstorms that might last a whole week.

Pluschow asked Lauezzari what lay beyond them.

'Nobody knows,' said his new friend. 'There is no one there and no way to get there.'

'They would know if they flew over them,' replied Gunther.

'Fly? That would be a crazy idea,' Lauezzari laughed.

'Well, I will know,' Gunther told him.

Chapter 19

Incredible and Savage Beauty

In the spring of 1926, Gunther Plüschow returned to Germany to write his second book, *Segelfahrt ins Wunderland* (Sail Journey in the Wonderland), an account of his trip to South America. At the same time he was planning a return to Patagonia and from the Plüschows' house in Heilbronner Strasse, in the Berlin district of Wilmersdorf, he wrote dozens of letters to leading German companies asking for sponsorship. One of the first to respond was the engine manufacturer, Deutz, and then others followed, most notably Ernst Heinkel, the aircraft designer who, four years earlier, had founded his own company based in Warnemünde on Germany's Baltic coast.

With the support of Germany's Communications and Transport Ministry, Heinkel provided Plüschow with a Heinkel HD24, basically a training seaplane. The pilot and trainee sat in open cockpits and the undercarriage consisted of twin pontoons. The BMW engine was fitted with a special carburettor to cope with the climatic challenges it would face. The aircraft would be called Tsingtau, although its nickname would be the *Silberkondor* – the Silver Condor.

Other organizations also provided equipment but one of Plüschow's greatest supporters was the Dr Karl Ullstein, the publisher who had brought out his first book and who now hoped for another bestseller after his appetite was whetted when Gunther showed him maps of the area he intended to visit. They were marked 'unexplored'.

Now the hero of Tsingtao needed a boat in which to make the journey. It was built at the Büsum shipyard of Kramer, Vagt & Beckmann on Germany's North Sea coast. The *Feuerland* was a

60ft ketch with a 50hp motor. The crew consisted of Plüschow himself; Paul Christiansen from Büsum, only 23 years old but already an experienced sailor, who would be Gunther's captain; Seppel Schmidt, from southern Bavaria, even younger at 21 but someone who already had experience of sailing around Cape Horn; Kurt Neubert, a 27-year-old cameraman from Dresden who was universally known as Garibaldi; cabin boy Harry Stoll, who took over from Karl Kolle when the 17-year-old from Bleckede on the Elbe left the *Feuerland* in Lisbon. Isot Plüschow, who would travel as far as Lisbon, was the cook and the *Feuerland*'s crew was completed by its mascot Schnauff, a dog presented to the expedition by a local automobile club.

One vital member of the team would not be on the *Feuerland*. Ernst Dreblow, the engineer, would travel with the Heinkel on the *Planet*, one of so-called Flying P-Liner sailing ships of the Hamburg-based Laeisz line that had given Plüschow his first taste of South America.

Born at Stettin on the Oder river in December 1892, Dreblow had trained as a mechanic at the shipyard there. Before the First World War he had spent a few weeks each year as a reservist at Kiel where he met Plüschow. After the war he had returned to Stettin where he graduated as an engineer and in 1921 accepted the offer of a job as a research engineer at the Askania works in Berlin where the company was making navigational equipment and timepieces for the burgeoning aircraft industry. He and Plüschow had met again at Johannisthal and when Gunther needed an experienced engineer for his expedition, Ernst Dreblow was the obvious choice.

On Sunday, 9 October 1927, the Büsum yard was decked out with flags and bunting for the naming ceremony of Plüschow's boat, an event supported by several local sailing clubs. The following month, at just after midday on 23 November and to the sounds of ships' sirens, the *Feuerland* left Büsum on the first leg of her voyage to the South Atlantic. Almost from the start, the party encountered bad weather but film of the journey seems to indicate that they remained in good heart. They called at

Madeira, the Canary Islands and the Cape Verde Islands before indulging in some high jinks as they crossed the Equator. Even poor Schnauff had to undergo the ritual before King Neptune and his Court.

In late July, the *Feuerland* called at Bahia State on the north-east coast of Brazil, where Plüschow travelled inland to film the Botocudos, as Europeans called the indigenous people who wore wooden disks or plugs in their lips and ears. At Blumenau, in the state of Santa Cruz, Plüschow addressed several German groups in a city that had been established by German immigrants in the mid-nineteenth century.

On 3 August 1928, the *Feuerland* docked at Buenos Aires where the party spent a few days. Then it was on towards Tierra del Fuego. On 21 October the *Feuerland* reached the Strait of Magellan and two days later was docking at Punta Arenas in Chile where Plüschow found Ernst Dreblow and the disassembled Heinkel waiting for him.

There was plenty of help at hand. Plüschow was greeted by Werner Gromsh, a professor at the German school in Punta Arenas, and by the governor of the Magellan Region and Chilean Antarctica. Local businesses were excited by the prospect of integrating their region with the rest of the South American continent and the hugely influential shipping company of Menéndez Behety had arranged for the expedition to bypass most of the red tape, while the Braun & Blanchard company that maintained a steamship service between Punta Arenas and Chile's Pacific Ocean ports provided an area in its repair yard for the reassembling of the Heinkel.

On the afternoon of Monday, 3 December 1928, the Heinkel was ready and Gunther Plüschow, with Ernst Dreblow his engineer, took off from Punta Arenas. First they flew over the community of Porvenir, founded by a strange mixture of Croatians and prospectors from the Los Lagos region of Chile during a nineteenth-century gold rush, and then crossed Dawson Island and the Darwin mountains before turning for Ushuaia – another candidate for the title of 'the southernmost city in the world' – on the Beagle Channel. As the Heinkel swooped down to land on the water at around 7.15pm, hundreds of curious locals came out to stare at perhaps the first aircraft they had ever seen. Plüschow presented an official with a bundle of letters – thereby delivering the first airmail ever to arrive in that part of the world – and was then entertained to dinner.

After a bad night's sleep, Gunther began the take-off back to Punta Arenas at around 5am but fierce head winds soon forced him back to Ushuaia before the aircraft ran out of fuel. On the following day Plüschow and Dreblow arrived back at Punta Arenas to something of a heroes' welcome.

Over the next few months, the pair continued their survey of Tierra del Fuego, taking hundreds of photographs and shooting hundreds of feet of cine film. The result was the first aerial pictures of the region, a hugely important and immensely fascinating body of work that is as astonishing today as it must have seemed to the people who first watched it eighty years ago. They returned to Ushuaia twice more, in January and February 1929, this time followed on each occasion by the *Feuerland* because, although the Heinkel was obviously the main player in all this, the *Feuerland* also had a central part as the tender to the floatplane. At the end of each day's aerial survey work, the *Silberkondor* would land off the coast and wait for the arrival of the *Feuerland* with supplies of fuel and other essential stores. Here, Plüschow tapped out his adventures on a Remington typewriter.

The ship also had a dark room in which the day's footage was developed and Plüschow's photographs did more than simply entertain people who had never seen the Tierra del Fuego from the air. In years to come they would help scientists studying the climate to compare changes in the glaciers. Plüschow also helped the young Chilean Air Force by compiling wind charts and meteorological tables, and after exploring the whole of Tierra del Fuego – in February 1929 he and Dreblow flew from Ushuaia to Cape Horn itself, widely considered to be the most southerly point of the South American continent at the tip of the archipelago – he turned his attentions north into Patagonia. One flight that must have given him exceptional pleasure was over the Torres del Paine, the two huge peaks that he had promised Richard Lauezzari he would one day conquer from the air.

Yet the adventure was coming to a close. In April 1929, word came from the Ullstein publishing house. They wanted Gunther Plüschow back in Germany. It was time for that next book.

Of his last flight before leaving he wrote:

The elongated land of Ultima Esperanza, smooth and peaceful like a mirror to the right of us, shrouded in grey mist and a brew of cloud, submerged under haze . . . I could just make out the outline of the wonderful Balmaceda [a small village in Chile, settled in the early part of the twentieth century by people expelled from Argentina when the border was settled]. To the left lay Puerto Natales, like a doll's city and now almost close enough to touch, in front of it the Bories refrigeration store . . . I looked at my watch, believing an eternity to have passed I found I had only been in the air 27 minutes. I circled around the tiny city of Natales a few times, circled the refrigeration store . . . where the *Silberkondor* was going to spend the quiet winter, saw to my satisfaction that there was a fast steamer ready to sail (hopefully going north). I put the engine into hover, like a dragonfly over the surface of the water. I believe today, for the first time, I have completed my 'masterflight'.

Funds were also running out and Plüschow had to help refinance his next expedition, so before he said goodbye to the rest of his colleagues, he sold the *Feuerland* to a Scotsman, John Hamilton, owner of sheep farms in both Patagonia and the Falkland Islands. Renamed *Penelope*, after Hamilton's daughter, the ketch, still crewed by Paul Christiansen and Seppel Schmidt who had been part of Plüschow's crew, would spend the next few years carrying sheep and horses around the Falklands, and plying back and forth to the Chilean mainland before several changes of

175

ownership, including being requisitioned by the Argentinean Navy during the Falklands War. Early in her new career the boat had returned to Patagonia to bring back a motley cargo of birds and animals, including skunks, rheas and otters, of which only the foxes and guanaco survived on the Falklands.

Of his own small animal kingdom, Plüschow handed his faithful mascot Schnauff to his old friend Lauezzari. It was Lauezzari who arranged for the body of the Heinkel to be stored at the giant refrigeration plant owned by the Sociedad Explotadora de Tierra del Fuego at Puerto Bories on the outskirts of Puerto Natales, 150 miles north-west of Punta Arenas on the shore of the Ultima Esperanza Sound. The aircraft's engine and instruments would accompany Plüschow back to Germany for repair.

In May 1929, in the late evening at the start of another southern winter, Gunther Plüschow shook hands with Ernst Dreblow, stepped aboard a steamship, and watched as the coast of Tierra del Fuego slipped from sight. Eight weeks later he was reunited with Isot and Guntolf, neither of whom he had seen for almost two years.

Back in Berlin, Plüschow began tidying up the manuscript of the book he had been typing on his Remington, and also began work on the film of his remarkable journey. Later that year, *Silberkondor Über Feuerland: Mit Segelkutter und Flugzeug ins Reich Meiner Träume* (Silver Condor over Tierra del Fuego: With Sail Cutter and Airplane in the Empire of My Dreams) was published to wide acclaim. At the same time the two-hour documentary film *Silberkondor Über Feuerland* was released to even wider applause. Plüschow is listed as the film's co-director along with Georg Victor Mendel, a well-known Berlin director with a string of films to his name. The music was by Willy Schmidt-Gentner, was one of the most successful German composers of film music in the history of German-language cinema.

In May 1930, Plüschow met the Spanish intellectual Armand Guerra, the filmmaker, screenwriter and actor who was working in Berlin at the Universum Film studios at Babelsberg. Guerra agreed to translate Gunther's second book into Spanish for the

South American market. A major figure in the fight against fascism, in 1932 Guerra would be expelled from Germany.

Of Gunther's film, Guerra later wrote:

Silberkondor Über Feuerland . . . has won a resounding success not only in Germany but in almost all European countries and recently in South America . . . a document full of emotions and indescribable beauty . . . delights the audience . . . a living document of priceless artistic and scientific value . . . an indescribable success.

In July 1930, Gunther Plüschow was ready to leave for South America once more. The success of both book and film had given him enough money to resume his travels and the film continued to generate income once he was there, although he found the political situation in Argentina had altered dramatically since his last visit: on 6 September 1930, in a military coup d'état, President Hipólito Yrigoyen had been ousted by the ultra-right wing General José Félix Uriburu. Initially, this made the granting of permissions difficult to obtain but eventually screenings in Buenos Aires, at the German Club and in the amphitheatre of the Faculty of Medicine at La Manzana de las Luces, proved enormously popular. When Plüschow moved on to Chile, to show the film in Santiago, he met with similar success. Even the Chilean dictator, Carlos Ibáñez del Campo, wanted to meet the famous aviator; one year later, Ibáñez was forced to flee as the effects of the world depression were felt in his country, although one day he would return.

These were circles that Plüschow must have enjoyed, not because he sympathized with the politics but because they recognized his status as an airman and explorer. It certainly smoothed the way for him to be granted permits to fly in both Argentina and Chile. For all the glory meant nothing if he could not resume the adventure in his 'land of incredible and savage beauty'.

Chapter 20

Final Flight

On 15 November 1930, Gunther Plüschow stood with Ernst Dreblow in a warehouse at Puerto Bories, looking down on a forlorn sight: in the eighteen months since Plüschow had been away, rats, attracted by a substance called isinglass which was obtained from the swim bladders of fish and used, among other things, for parchment conservation, had eaten into the wings of the *Silberkondor*. The crossbar of the left wing was particularly badly damaged and major repairs would be needed if the aircraft were to fly again. At first they considered sending to Germany for spare parts but the cost and the long delay meant that it was not a viable option. And so they set to work, putting in long shifts to make the Heinkel airworthy once more. Just before Christmas, the *Silberkondor* was ready and the adventure could resume.

The plan was to continue filming more of the Southern Patagonian Ice Field but several flights took them over the particular area that Plüschow had visited with Richard Lauezzari in 1926. Gunther seemed forever drawn back to the spectacular granite spires and mountains of the massif. On one occasion bad weather forced him to land the Heinkel on Sarmiento Lake in what would, thirty years later, become the Torres del Paine National Park. The lake had been named after a Spanish explorer, Pedro Sarmiento de Gamboa; when Plüschow and Dreblow were forced to spend several days in a small cove on its shores, they dubbed their camping ground 'Tsingtau Cove'.

The men were settled well enough at their base at Cerro Guido, but the Chilean authorities now wanted to inspect the dilapidated-looking Heinkel to ensure that it met safety standards. There were also rumours circulating that the Germans

179

were not simply surveying the area for scientific purposes but were in fact on an espionage mission for their government. Plüschow went so far as to publicly deny this, but to avoid a confrontation he and Dreblow moved into Argentinean territory, to Ensenada Rico in the province of Santa Cruz.

Gunther sent back dozens of newspaper and magazine articles to Germany. Towards the end of the year the Berlin-based *Vossische Zeitung*, generally regarded as the German national newspaper of record, which had been taken over by the Ullstein publishing house in 1914, reported that Plüschow was setting up camp on the shores of Lake Viedma which flowed into Lake Argentino, the biggest lake in Argentina with a surface area of 566 square miles, through La Leona River

The filming continued, thousands of feet of film in fact, as Plüschow and Dreblow soared over the desolate region when better weather made the flights all the more enjoyable but, as January wore on, fierce north-west winds coming from the Pacific Ocean combined with the winds off the ice field to cause downwinds that smashed on the *Silberkondor*. There were few days when repairs of some sort were not necessary and a critical lack of spare parts greatly hampered Dreblow in his attempts to keep the Heinkel airborne. Now camped at El Calfate, a hamlet that was not much more than a place of shelter for wool traders, the pair felt that to finance future expeditions they had to keep flying. They had to take risks.

Dreblow was under particular pressure because the Heinkel's engine was being damaged by its continual exposure to extremely low air temperatures. Both men were also exhausted but a mutual respect and trust, built up from months of sharing so many hardships, maintained their relationship where others might have foundered.

At midnight on 20 January 1931, a fierce storm drove the Heinkel up on to the shore of Lake Argentino. Soaked to the skin, Plüschow and Dreblow spent several hours getting the aircraft back into the water. That work done, when they returned to their camp they found that their tent had been washed away and their belongings strewn about. It was all but soul-destroying.

Four days later, the Heinkel's engine refused to lift them over a mountain range and they were saved only by a wind that picked them up like a giant hand. Gunther recorded in his diary: 'What I have lived and seen no one can take away from me.' It seems that he knew he was probably living on borrowed time.

On Monday, 26 January, yet another fierce storm forced Plüschow to land the Heinkel in a small body of water less than a mile long, only 300yds wide and set between two walls of rock each over 2,000ft high. It was a virtual prison. To compound matters, one of the Heinkel's pontoons had struck a rock and cracked. Water had entered it and destroyed the fuel cans and food stored there. The crossbar on the left wing – the one so badly damaged by rodents when the *Silberkondor* was in storage – had been damaged again, this time when the aircraft hit the surface at an angle. Braving the icy water, Plüschow worked for almost six hours to repair the pontoon, while Dreblow worked on the crossbar.

Then Plüschow began to explore their prison, trying to find a way out through the large masses of ice. Sometime after midday he made several attempts to take off, each one aborted because of strong winds that blew not only head on at the *Silberkondor* but also pushed down on it. As darkness fell, the idea was abandoned altogether and Plüschow and Dreblow tried to find some shelter from the storm, and salvage any food that had not been ruined by the spilled aviation fuel.

On the morning of Wednesday, 28 January 1931 they tried again. The alternative would be almost certain death from cold and starvation.

After Plüschow had first cruised slowly around the narrow inlet, pushing ice to one side, the *Silberkondor* rose into the air and then was free. Gunther turned the Heinkel towards the south-east and their base at El Calfate.

At about 2pm (some witnesses give the time as up to an hour earlier), several farm workers cutting wood on the southern shore of Brazo Rico, a lake connected to Lake Argentino some 40 miles from El Calfate, heard the sound of an aircraft. They looked up and saw it about 2 miles away, flying at a height of between 1,100ft and 1,600ft (again depending on witnesses). The aircraft began to wobble and tilt. Then two light-coloured shapes fell from it and the aeroplane, now almost vertical, followed them down.

It was 4.30pm by the time local officials reached the lake. About 200ft inland from the shore they found two bodies. Documents in the clothing of one included Argentinean and Chilean civilian pilot's licences in the name of Gunther Plüschow; he was not quite 45. The other body was identified as Ernst Dreblow. An unopened parachute lay nearby. Out in the water was the wreckage of an aircraft on which was painted the word 'Tsingtau'.

Epilogue

In late February 1931 the bodies of Gunther Plüschow and Ernst Dreblow were exhumed from their temporary graves and taken to Buenos Aires on board the Menéndez Behety shipping company's steamer *Asturiano* that docked in the Argentinean capital on 4 March. The remains were cremated opposite the national cemetery, better known as the Chacarita where many famous Argentineans have been laid to rest, and the ashes sent via Hamburg to Berlin. On 16 May 1931, with great ceremony, the urns were interred at the Park Cemetery in the suburb of Lichterfelde, although four years later Ernst Dreblow's ashes were moved to the Protestant Cemetery in Rathenow, about 45 miles west of Berlin.

The crash site was surveyed by Rufino Luro Cambacérès, one of the pioneers of aviation in Argentina; Cambacérès, a pilot with the Argentinean Naval Reserve, had apparently suggested mounting a rescue attempt when it was discovered that Plüschow and Dreblow were missing.

An official inquiry into the deaths found both to have been accidental. It was not clear whether the damage to the Heinkel was caused when Plüschow was forced to land it in that icy prison, or whether it suffered further damage as it escaped. Some accounts say that the men's parachutes did not open, others that they bailed out clutching parachutes that were torn from their hands. One month after the crash it was reported that an American citizen scouring the crash site had come across a gold chain and medallion bearing the figure '13' – Isot's gift to Gunther all those years before.

Gunther Plüschow was the proverbial legend in his own life-time and his end in the most tragic of circumstances made it was inevitable that the legend would grow even stronger. After his death two new films were released. In 1931, *Fahrt ins Land der Wunder und Wolken* (Journey into the Land of Wonders and Clouds) came out, to be followed in 1932 by *Ikarus – Gunther Plüschow's Fliegerschicksal* (Icarus – Gunther Plüschow's Airman's Destiny). In 1933, Isot Plüschow's biography of her husband – *Gunther Plüschow, deutscher Seemann und Flieger: Das Bild seines Lebens* (Gunther Plüschow, German Sailor and Airman: The Picture of his Life) – was published by Ullstein. When Isot died in Berlin on 1 August 1979, aged 90, she was buried in the grave that held her husband's ashes. The Plüschows' son, Guntolf, who took his father's first name, emigrated to Canada and in 2007 was living in Winnipeg.

Like Gunther senior, the *Feuerland* also entered into legend. In August 2006, almost eighty years after she had carried him to Tierra del Fuego, the *Feuerland*, now reverted to her original name, returned to Büsum after being purchased by Bernd Buchner who was first officer on a cruise ship when he first set eyes on her in the Falklands. The original plan had been for the *Feuerland* to make the return journey under her own power but instead she had to be loaded on to the container ship *Monte Cervantes* and taken first to Hamburg. The *Feuerland* eventually arrived back at her birthplace towed by the lifeboat cruiser *Hans Hackmack*. She was a sad sight and work began on restoring her. The *Silberkondor*'s crankshaft – 5ft long and weighing 110lbs – is preserved in Argentina's National Aeronautics Museum.

It all adds up to a remarkable legacy. But how much of Gunther Plüschow's story is actually true? A lone airman in a flimsy damaged aircraft with improvised repairs going into conflict twice a day against a far superior Japanese force without being shot down? It sounds incredible.

His astonishing journey to Shanghai, then all the way across America, and then a daring escape from a British mainland prisoner of war camp – the only German soldier to do so and make it all the way home in either world war – is all breathtaking stuff.

And then the final chapters of a remarkable life: exploring some of the most inhospitable parts of our planet before meeting a cruel but perhaps inevitable fate – a mishap in the air.

It all reads like a derring-do boys' adventure book.

So, again: how much of it is true? The answer is almost certainly – almost every last bit of it. True, Gunther Plüschow appears to have been something of a showman, a man with an eye for a headline-catching story. So it is not beyond the bounds of possibility that the occasional detail was exaggerated or shifted around in the interests of literary licence; like, perhaps, the 40-mile round trip that he said he made walking from Gravesend to London and back in one day when he was wearing wet clothes and must have been absolutely exhausted in the first place. And when he left Puerto Natales for home in 1929, according to Plüschow, most of the town turned up to wave him off. It may well have happened.

The only real doubt appears to be the claim that he shared in a world record altitude flight with Otto Linnekogel; the previous year Georges Legagneux had recorded a greater height, an event that was well documented at the time. Linnekogel's and Plüschow's feat was a German record – why let that get in the way of an even better story?

But Plüschow did fly daily against the Japanese at Tsingtao, although if he is sometimes described as a First World War 'flying ace' then it paints very misleading picture because Gunther Plüschow was no Red Baron beating the odds against the Royal Flying Corps over the Western Front. That was not his brief. In Tsingtao his absolute priority was to keep the Taube in one piece in order to continue his vital reconnaissance flights. But did he, as he claimed, become the first pilot in history to shoot down another aircraft in air-to-air combat? There were no witnesses, of course, but he would probably have received a rocket from his commanding officer if he had admitted it at the time. And there is, albeit flimsy, circumstantial evidence that a Japanese pilot was shot down in those first few weeks of the war. Who else would have done it, if not Gunther Plüschow?

That he did escape from Britain and make his own way back to Germany is a fact. And he did sail all the way from Germany

185

to the southernmost tip of South America. And he did fly for hundreds upon hundreds of dangerous hours in the most appalling weather conditions before being killed when his *Silberkondor* finally gave up.

Even in 1931, aviation science was relatively primitive. So let us not forget that when Plüschow was flying over Kiaochow in 1914 – and having to be 'slung-shot' into the air and then slowed down on his return by the use of two sandbags and a rope – it was only eleven years after the Wright brothers had achieved the world's first controlled, powered and sustained heavier-than-air human flight. It took a particular brand of courage to face the many hazards of flying the Taube, never mind being shot at by the enemy at the same time.

Was he a spy? There have been stories that when he was in England in 1913 he was gathering intelligence for the Imperial German government; and that when he was flying over Patagonia in the late 1920s and early 1930s he was filming the Chile–Argentina border for the Weimar government who secretly part-financed the trip. Well, it is difficult to imagine Gunther Plüschow as an operative, although the region had a German presence, was an important trading area and it would be unsurprising if his government had asked him to supply information that he would have gathered anyway. At the time, the Chileans certainly seemed have suspected that his sympathies lay with Argentina, although that did not prevent them from later honouring his memory.

As a former military hero he might well have been courted by the emerging right-wing forces that eventually took over Germany, but above all Gunther Plüschow, while a patriot, was definitely his own man, so it is equally difficult to imagine that he would have been sucked into the Hitler years. Indeed, as the Nazi Party increased its influence in Germany it seems that Plüschow, such a free spirit, wanted nothing to do with it. His friendship with such a prominent anti-fascist as Armand Guerra certainly suggests that he would have had no time for Adolf Hitler and his madmen.

Above all, one forms the impression that Gunther Plüschow was a clubbable man, a ladies man, someone to whom the lone adventure was the most important thing of all. He was certainly made of 'The Right Stuff'. All in all, he seem to have been a larger-than-life character who, had he not existed, someone would have had to invent. Fortunately, there was no need. Gunther Plüschow was real enough.

In February 1931, writing in the magazine *Popular Film*, Armand Guerra wrote that during the course of translating Gunther Plüschow's work into Spanish, he had come to form a great friendship with Plüschow who had invited the filmmaker to join him on his next trip to Patagonia. Guerra had to decline because of commitments in Berlin. But, he said, he would dearly liked to have accepted.

Guerra ended his tribute: 'Rest in peace, dear friend. The world will honour your work.'

Principal Sources

Books

Bennett, Geoff, *The Pepper Trader: True Tales of the German East Asia Squadron and the Man Who Cast Them in Stone*, London, Equinox Publishing, 2006.

Boyne, Walter, J, *Air Warfare: An International Encyclopedia*, Santa Barbara, CA, ABC Clio, 2002.

Clemente, Steven E, *For King and Kaiser! The Making of the Prussian Army Officer, 1860–1914*, Westport, CT, Greenwood Press, 1992.

Dove, Richard (ed.), *Totally Un-English? Britain's Internment of 'Enemy Aliens' in Two World Wars* Amsterdam and New York, Yearbook of the Research Centre for German and Austrian Exile Studies, vol. 7, 2005.

Fairbank, John K, and Twitchett, Denis (eds), *The Cambridge History of China*, Cambridge, Cambridge University Press, 1986.

Fryer, Hazel, and Squires, Anthony, *The Gothic Taste: Humphrey Repton and the Development of Donington Park*, Leicester, Leicestershire Archaeological and Historical Society 70, 1996.

Hoyt, Edwin P, *The Fall of Tsingtao*, London, Arthur Barker, 1975.

Jones, Jefferson, *The Fall of Tsingtau, with a Study of Japan's Ambitions in China*, Boston and New York, Mifflin, 1915.

Litvachkes, Roberto, *Gunther Plüschow: Una vida de sueños, aventuras y desafíos por un amor imposible. La Patagonia*, Buenos Aires, Serie Del-Sur, 2006.

Plüschow, Gunther, *Die Abenteuer des Fliegers von Tsingtau*, Berlin, Ullstein, 1917.

Plüschow, Gunther, *Segelfahrt ins Wunderland. Im Reiche der Papageien und Guanakos*, Berlin, Deutscher Verlag, 1926.

Plüschow, Gunther, *Silberkondor Über Feuerland: Mit Segelkutter und Flugzeug ins Reich Meiner Träume*, Berlin, Ullstein, 1929.

Plüschow, Isot, *Gunther Plüschow, deutscher Seemann und Flieger: Das Bild seines Lebens*, Berlin, Ullstein, 1933.

van Emden, Richard, and Humphries, Steve, *All Quiet on the Home Front*, London, Headline, 2003.

von Salomon, Ernst, *Die Kadetten*, Berlin, Deutsche Buch-Gemeinschaft, 1933.

Whittaker, Robert E., *Dragon Master: The Kaiser's One-Man Airforce in Tsingtau, China, 1914*, Cleveland, WI, Compass Books, 1994.

Gunther Plüschow

Newspapers
Daily Mail
Daily Sketch
Derby Evening Telegraph
Leicester Mercury
Leicester Evening Mail
New York Times
Staffordshire Sentinel
The Times
Washington Post

News Agencies
Mercopress South Atlantic New Agency

Archives
The National Archives, Kew, UK

Films
Silberkondor Über Feuerland

Index